THE SONY TAPE

ROCK

REVIEW

First published in Great Britain by
Rambletree Publishing
Chancery House,
319 City Road,
London EC1V 1LJ

in association with

Pelham Books
44 Bedford Square
London WC1B 3DU

The Sony Tape Rock Review GS.
  1. Rock music — History and criticism
  I. Jones, Lesley-Ann
  II. Eggar, Robin   III. Swern, Phil
  784. 5'4   ML3534

ISBN 0-947894-00-4

Edited, designed and produced by First Editions
Typeset by Presentia Arts, Horsham
Origination by D S Colour International
Printed by Redwood Burn, Trowbridge, England.

THE SONY TAPE
ROCK REVIEW

EDITED BY
LESLEY-ANN JONES, ROBIN EGGAR & PHIL SWERN

RAMBLETREE
PELHAM

Unravelling the Mysteries of Audio Cassettes

Highly computerised recording studios, sophisticated microphones, digital recording techniques. Just some of the advances in sound recording techniques that have been developed in recent years and have become an accepted part of today's rock industry.

However, just as sound recording techniques have improved by leaps and bounds in the past decade, so too has there been a need for advances in sound reproduction qualities. Nowadays, the sound you can hear through your Hi-Fi system at home, comes closer than ever to matching exactly the sound put down in the recording studio.

But the quality of sound you hear at home does not just depend on the sophistication of the equipment on

which you play your records and tapes, but also on the quality of the software you use. After all, even the highest of Hi-Fi cannot disguise the scratches or warps from a badly damaged LP. Similarly a poor quality cassette will not do justice to the reproduction abilities of a good stereo system. Conversely, a good quality audio tape will maximise the sound qualities of even today's budget priced or low feature cassette recorders.

How to chose a quality tape though – that's the question. Wander into any good tape stockist and you are immediately confronted with a mind-boggling choice of brand names, tape types, lengths and multipacks. A look at the packaging hardly helps to narrow down the choice. Words and phrases like Type 1, Ferric Chrome, Dynamic Range and Minimum Output level, only serve to confuse the average purchaser still further. In the end, understandably, and with a shrug of resignation, he normally plumps for a brand he knows at a price that seems about right. But by doing this he may not be making the choice that would best suit his equipment or his recording purposes.

A few simple guidelines can help to unravel some of the mysteries.

Basically there are four 'Types' of audio tapes:

Type 1 – Ferric
Type 2 – Chrome
Type 3 – Ferrichrome
Type 4 – Metal

In simple terms the 'type' of tape refers to the substance or chemicals from which that tape is made. And, again as a rule, the further you go up the scale from Type 1 to Type 4, the better the quality of tape you will get. That is, the

sound recorded on a Type 4 tape will more exactly reproduce the original sound than a tape of any other type.

But before we all rush off and invest in metal type tapes, we should be aware that naturally these will cost us more. Not only that, but it may be that the demands of our cassette-playing equipment do not warrant the sophistication of reproduction that a metal tape will give. Even the so-called 'basic' Type 1 tapes of today have advanced so much, that provided they are made by one of the leading names, they will prove adequate for many general recording needs.

(Incidentally, Ferrichrome tapes are rarely found nowadays, since the performance of chrome tapes is now so good that there is only a limited need for this specialised Type 3 cassette.)

Sony have been at the forefront of developments of many of the recent advances in both sound equipment and tape technology. Their audio cassettes have won praise and awards from independent judges as being the best quality tapes you can buy. But they have recently introduced a range of new tapes which take those advances still further.

Sony HF is a Type 1 tape and has been specifically designed to cover the need for a general purpose cassette for music and speech recording. It is as at home in your mono cassette recorder, as it is in a dictating machine or your walkman.

Sony HF-S answers the need for superior music reproduction, and is the ideal partner for stereo cassette radios and music centres.

Sony UCX is tailored to suit the more demanding performance of the Hi-Fi system, and is a Type 2 tape with the Chrome properties now favoured by leading Record Companies.

But if your Hi-Fi set-up is even more demanding, then look at **Sony UCX-S** tape, combining chrome-tape performance with even greater capabilities.

And finally for the live or digital reproduction required by today's recording studios, and in order to get the most out of today's top Hi-Fi systems, why settle for less than **Sony Metal-ES** tape, the ultimate expression of "state of the art" performance and the standard by which other tapes should be judged. In fact, since its launch in Japan, it has already been acclaimed by leading authorities as quite simply the best performing audio cassette in the world.

Whatever your requirements of sound reproduction, it can be infuriating to find that the mechanical design of the cassette does not live up to the performance of the tape itself. That's why, whichever Sony Tape you choose, you'll find it features the unique SP2 mechanism, which removes the risk of jamming or tape unravelling – as well as eliminating capstan squeaks.

After all, when you're recording sounds as good as those available today, the last thing you want to hear is the sound of the cassette!

FOREWORD

- **by Bill Wyman of the Rolling Stones**

The phrase 'here today, gone tomorrow' might have been coined for the rock world. Bands come and go, but so do fashions, hairstyles, attitudes. The anarchic punk reaction to the love and peace of the hippy era was an exciting but short-lived moment in rock history. When it's all over and the fan magazines and posters have been trashed, there's very little left to remind you of that time in your life.

So what a good idea to have an annual rock review which in words and pictures captures the essence of a year. This book really does tell you what's happening now. The editors come from all sides of the media — Lesley-Ann Jones from television, Robin Eggar from Fleet Street and Phil Swern from radio. They have put together a team of top journalists and personalities, including Alan Freeman, Anne Nightingale, Malcolm Garrett and Peter Wagg, to produce colourful profiles of the top 30 acts and fascinating feature articles on current trends. They tell you about the stars and the people behind the scenes — from Michael Jackson to Culture Club's producer Steve Levine. At a time when the way a band looks is just as important as how it sounds, the writers present the current image and style.

All in all, this is a book you will enjoy reading now and go back to again and again in years to come.

THE ROCK REVIEW

TOP 30

Big Country	Frankie	Cyndi Lauper	Lionel Richie	Thompson Twins
Elvis Costello	Heaven 17	Limahl	Sade	U2
Culture Club	Human League	Madness	Simple Minds	UB40
Depeche Mode	Michael Jackson	New Order	The Smiths	Wham
Duran Duran	Howard Jones	The Police	Spandau Ballet	The Womacks
Eurythmics	Nik Kershaw	The Pretenders	Style Council	Paul Young

If it was U2 who made the connection between post-punk exploration and the undying potency of good old rock, it was Big Country who turned that notion into super-simplified functionalism. Formed by erstwhile Skids guitarist Stuart Adamson (born April 11, 1958), from Dunfermline, Big Country shot to stardom in Britain and America on the back of a winning formula comprising Celtic whimsy fuelled by vast guitar chords.

The group's own biography speaks (apparently with a straight face) of *"men who had done enough wandering to know their true goals and saw them in a Big Country, this led to a great coming together of cultures which was a joy to behold and once again the people were strong and happy . . ."* Farcical, but efficacious.

B·I·G C·O·U·N·T·R·Y

The facts of the matter were these. Adamson, a man much given to ruminating on the benefits of family, friends and community, was fed up to the back teeth of trying to work alongside berserk vocalist/pseudo poet Richard Jobson in The Skids. The Skids had once performed what Adamson memorably described as *"theme tunes for war movies and romantic losers"*, but Jobson was increasingly turning the group into a form of absurdist performance art. Adamson, who preferred rock music, left.

Back home in Fife with pregnant wife Sandra, Adamson spent the latter half of 1981 writing songs and combing the neighbourhood for people to play them with. *"The only guideline we set down was to make the band as honest as we can, so that we could cut out all the bullshit that goes on in the audience-star relationship,"* said Adamson – hardly a revolutionary sentiment, but indicative at least of his desire to create a new niche for himself.

Adamson swiftly recruited second guitarist Bruce Watson (born March 11, 1961), who lived just across the railway tracks, but other personnel proved more difficult to find. Still, Phonogram were sufficiently impressed with Adamson's new songs to invite him and Watson to London to record some demo tapes. Fortuitously, the pair brought bassman Tony Butler (born February 13, 1957) and drummer Mark Brzezicki (born June 21, 1957) along to the studio as hired guns, and found that the collective musical chemistry was an immediate success.

Butler and Brzezicki had once been in a group called On The Air with Simon Townshend, played on sessions with Simon's better-known brother Pete, and can also be heard on The Pretenders' best single **Back On The Chain Gang**. Butler was offered a full-time job with The Pretenders, but the mortality rate put him off. Both were impressed enough by their sessions with Adamson to throw in their lot with this new band, though Brzezicki insisted on a clause in his contract which leaves him free to tackle session work. A week, after all, is a long time in rock'n'roll.

In October 1982, after playing some live shows which gave early notice of Big Country's considerable onstage potential, they released their first single, **Harvest Home**. It had been produced by Chris Thomas, but he'd had problems getting the best out of the band in the studio. Adamson's voice, in particular, had been a bone of contention, with Thomas trying to camouflage weaknesses under a barrage of overdubs. Nevertheless, **Harvest Home** indicated what Big Country were after. The skirling guitars were already present and correct, as was a lyric of suitably mock-Biblical portent. *"Just as ye sow, ye shall reap",* chorused the band, a pronouncement scarcely grammatical, but nevertheless groaning with significance. It was only rock'n'roll, but you could pretend it was philosophy — if you were drunk enough. The visual imagery was already established, too — tartan shirts and baggy working man's dungarees. It looked completely casual and was obviously the product of painstaking calculation.

To get the equation absolutely right, a new producer was clearly top of the list. Steve Lillywhite, U2's studio mentor, looked a likely candidate, and so it proved. Big Country's next single was **Fields Of Fire**, a better record all round. Off went those guitars again (frequently compared with bagpipes), back came the

are not supposed to be a comedy turn, mention must be made of the noble **Chance,** a song about a busted marriage featuring a lovely melody and a fine surge of power towards the fade. It deservedly became the group's next hit single.

Meanwhile, the Americans were

Adamson had by now perfected a winning line in Very Sincere Blarney for the press. It was near enough to the God, home and apple pie philosophy as makes no difference. For instance: *"As far as I'm concerned, people who buy our records or come to our gigs are as much a part of the group as us. Without them, there wouldn't be a Big Country . . . If there is a future in music, it has got to come through young people being shown that you can express yourself honestly through music."* Or again: *"It's at times like this that the most vital music is made, when people feel a lack and a want and a need for someone who can go*

familiar Highland-fling chord sequences, Adamson sang it loud and clear, and last but certainly not least was The Steve Lillywhite Drum Sound, and awesome creation. **Fields** remains Big Country's best out-and-out rocker, especially live. The follow-up, **In A Big Country,** was almost identical but did worse in the charts.

July '83 brought the band's debut album, **The Crossing,** again with Lillywhite at the helm. It was a mixed bag. The singles were there, alongside more expansive pieces like **Porrohman** as well as a generous helping of absolute old tosh like **The Storm** and **1000 Stars.** The artwork, lyrics and Boy's Own bravado of the music suggested a thoroughly unlikely mixture of Robert Louis Stephenson, Robbie Burns and Biggles, with Adamson's knack for turning faintly-remembered poetry into utter doggerel knowing no bounds — *"The storm broke upon us with fury and flame. Both horses and masters bogged down in the rain"* **(The Storm).**

However, lest we forget that Big Country

clamouring for some of this righteous stuff, which Big Country were delighted to give them. The land of Coca-Cola succumbed with ludicrous ease. Obviously Big Country's tartan shirts (now augmented by matching scarves) had considerable export potential, while their thunderous guitars and strings of interchangeable songs evidently reminded Americans of many of their own best-loved outfits.

up there and say how they're feeling and not be scared of the consequences."

This was sententious rubbish in anybody's language, and Big Country accordingly became a fixture in the US charts (album and singles). According to the Los Angeles Times, *"this truly is a band with a future and a heart as big as its name".* To prove it, the band's New Year's Eve show in Glasgow at the end of 1983 was broadcast on America's hugely influential cable TV channel, MTV. The boys had arrived. During the summer they headed off to Abba's studio in Sweden, once again with Lillywhite, attempting to accomplish one of rock's most difficult tasks — a good second album.

Big Country are essentially a stirring live band, who play an instantly recognisable and very limited form of hard rock. They deserve credit for refining form and function into a blindingly simple package, but their homespun men-of-the-people image is as much a sales pitch as a guiding philosophy. They'll probably be around for years.

● Bruce Watson, Stuart Adamson, Tony Butler and Mark Brzezicki

ELVIS

Elvis Costello was the unlikeliest hero from the New Wave era of 1977. Bespectacled and sickly looking, he was about as far from a rock star as it was possible to get.

But with a combination of inspired judgement, fierce commitment, faultless taste, and sheer inspiration, he has become the consummate artist. He has constantly broken new ground with total confidence and immense style, seemingly unwilling to remain working in the same musical confines for too long.

He has developed into one of rock's most articulate and challenging songwriters; comfortable and impressive across a wide spectrum of contemporary music. Armed with the muscle and quality of his backing group The Attractions, few can match the intensity and class he brings to both live appearances and records.

He was born Declan McManus in Liverpool on August 25, 1955. He was the son of dance band singer Ross McManus – for many years the backbone of Britain's ever popular Joe Loss Orchestra. Little is known of his past since he prefers to shroud it in mystery. What is clear is that he was restless with ambition.

During the day he programmed computers for cosmetics giant Elizabeth Arden. In his free time he was busy writing tunes, recording demos, trying to get his songs played on the radio and looking for a contract with a label.

One day in June 1976, unannounced and unknown, he walked into the fledgling offices of Stiff Records – a new independent label with a roster headed by Nick Lowe – and was signed up immediately.

With London erupting with the fury of punk and Stiff glowing with their ties to 'man of the hour' Graham Parker, it was an easy marriage. Young Declan had produced an utterly original fusion with his astute and trained musical mind. He'd played off the bittersweet tenderness of jazz, the self-pity of country and western and the vitriolic contempt of rock'n'roll. The Stiff executives heard the passion of punk and the craft of Parker in his songs.

Rechristened Elvis Costello in a jest that quickly turned sour – after Presley's death, a switch of names was seriously considered – he was put in the studio with Lowe and Californian country-rock band Clover.

The result was three arresting and imaginative singles, **Less Than Zero, Alison** and **The Angels Want To Wear My Red Shoes** in 1977 and a stunning album, **My Aim Is True,** which reached Number 14 in the charts. Both the public and the media were universal in their acclaim.

In June 1977 The Attractions were formed – Pete Thomas (drums), Bruce Thomas (bass) and Steve Nieve (keyboards). The rest of the year was spent touring, notably with the Live Stiffs package, which included Ian Dury, Wreckless Eric, Larry Wallis and Nick Lowe. A fourth single, **Watching The Detectives,** a bubbling brew of reggae and malevolence, reached Number 15.

Early 1978 saw a change of label to Radar - owned by manager Jake Riveria (Andrew Jakeman). His first single for them, **(I Don't Want To Go To) Chelsea,** reached Number 16 and his second album, **This Year's Model,** entered the album chart at Number Four and remained on the listings for four months.

The rest of the year was taken up with frenzied touring and the recording of his third album **Armed Forces.** It entered the charts at Number Two and drew

ELVIS

COSTELLO

COSTELLO

country album – in Nashville under the watchful eye of Billy Sherrill as producer in May 1981. The collection of country standards and personal favourites won critical and commercial acclaim, despite the fact that Sherrill – a Nashville legend – didn't take the project seriously. **Good Year For The Roses** reached Number Six, while **Sweet Dreams** also charted.

January 1982 saw Costello and The Attractions at the Albert Hall, backed by the full might of the 92-piece Royal Philharmonic Orchestra, on a virtual full run-through of his career to date.

The Spring of 1982 he released what has been his most cohesive work to date **Imperial Bedroom**. But it was noticeable that as Costello craft became further and further refined, so the commercial appeal of his work waned. Despite coming top in virtually every poll worldwide the album sold relatively poorly.

He was given to collaborations: he produced Scots pop band The Bluebells and wrote one of the most devasting singles of the eighties with Madness producer Clive Langer. His song **Shipbuilding** was a hit in 1983 for Robert Wyatt – nearly a year after its release. It dealt in a poignant and articulate way with the far reaching effects of a modern day crusade like the Falklands War.

1983 saw further legal wrangles which prevented the release of the **Punch The Clock** album. But Elvis felt the single **Pills and Soap** couldn't wait and put it out under the name of The Imposter. It became his biggest hit for ages reaching the top 20.

Punch The Clock was a far more

ELVIS COSTEL

breathless admiration from the media at the beginning of 1979.

Listeners' first impressions were not of the savage lyricism. It was the sheer sound: an intricate roar of rock, propelled by echoed drums and an insistent Farfisa organ. It produced an undertow that drew the audience into the heart of Costello's vision.

The songs depicted life as a nightmare of personal contacts that seem like a haven, but become an intimate extension of the web society has spun to imprison.

Because his personal relations are perceived as a metaphor for relations in society, he managed to transcend the petty spitefulness of lesser rock stars. He was obsessed with the reality of domination.

It was this concern that led him to appear at rallies against racism in Britain. It was totally out of character when he reviled Ray Charles as a *"Blind, ignorant nigger"*, during a drunken

argument with singer Bonnie Bramlett, in an American bar. It was an outburst that was to take away some of his American support and hung like a cloud over his transatlantic dealings.

During the same year he had his biggest British single **Oliver's Army** (Number Two in the chart) and still managed to find time to produce The Specials' first album.

Again, legal dealings held up his fourth album **Get Happy**. The single **I Can't Stand Up For Falling Down** was released on F Beat in February 1980 and reached Number Four and the album attained Number Two.

Trust was released at the beginning of 1981. It was voted as his best to date, and was particularly noted for his pronounced vocal abilities, fearless experimentation with rock conventions and its brilliant sustained lyrical attack.

He diversified even further when he and The Attractions recorded **Almost Blue** – a

accessible album and utilised a brasher power with the use of the TKO horn section.

The Imposter raised his mysterious head in the spring of 1984 with **Peace In Our Time** – a minor hit.

Costello released another album, **Goodbye Cruel World** in the summer of '84. Earlier that year he toured the States accompanied only by his guitar with the kind of rapturous praise not initially accorded to the album. While the remake of Ricky Nelson's **I Wanna Be Loved** cracked the top 30, he began an acting career in the TV series *Scully*.

What is clear is that Costello's aim has been consistently true. His songs have been covered by artists as diverse as George Jones and Linda Ronstadt. He has proved himself to be one of the most durable of the New Wave talents, as well as probably the most skillful. One day he'll make a duff album – but I wouldn't bet on it.

Culture C

June 14, 1984. Scores of popular newspapers all over the world carry a front-page picture of a celebrity, together with his lifesize image that's about to be placed in Madame Tussaud's famous waxworks museum in London.

He hardly needs identifying – but with two of him in the same shot, pun-hungry sub-editors can't resist: *"Oh Boy, Oh Boy!"* screams *The Sun*; *"Twin Boys"* quips the *Daily Mirror*. The celebrity is Culture Club's lead singer Boy George, and this tribute to his fame takes place on his 23rd birthday.

The origins of Culture Club go back to 1981, when Mikey Craig spotted a picture of George (then Lieutenant Lush) and Annabella Lwin in a music paper. Mikey had for some time been determined to pursue his musical ambitions, while at the same time coping with the pressures of impoverished parenthood. George had long been an outrageous and ubiquitous presence in the nightclubs of London, Birmingham and elsewhere; now he was doing a brief spell as joint vocalist with Annabella in Bow Wow Wow.

The picture Mikey spotted came with a story suggesting that Malcolm McLaren (then manager of Bow Wow Wow) wanted to form a separate band for George. In truth, George and McLaren could not get on and George left, planning to form his own band. George and Mikey recruited John Suede on guitar, called themselves The Sex Gang Children and started looking for a drummer. At the suggestion of his friend Kirk Brandon, George phoned ex-Clash/Damned/Ants drummer Jon Moss.

The contact between Jon, who loathed the New Romantic Scene and describes himself as *"a bit of a puritan"*, and supreme nightclub poseur George was decisive in laying the foundations for Culture Club's success. In contrast with many of his previous bands, Jon found that his own musical contribution was both welcome and expected. George found a good musician with long and varied experience of the music business, and with just the right cool and organised mind to offset his own rather more volatile approach. Mikey, whose bass provided a powerful reggae/funk influence, had found the makings of a band that was capable of turning his pop ambitions into reality. At Jon's urging, they changed the band's name to Culture Club and when Suede was replaced by Roy Hay from Essex, the band were ready to start developing their music and style. A chance visit by Virgin Publishing's Danny Goodwin to one of the band's first concerts, at Crocs club in Rayleigh, led eventually to their recording contract with Virgin Records.

In just two years, Culture Club became established as one of the world's most popular bands and identified with a global revival of British pop. Their first two singles in the Summer of 1982, however, failed to make an impact on the UK charts, and by the time they released their third, **Do You Really Want To Hurt Me?** some reviewers were already writing them off. *"Third time lucky for George and the boys? Don't think so, this is weak watered down fourth division reggae,"* opined one, while another said that *"the shallow, anorexic white rasta riddums fail to ignite any real spark of passion."*

They were wrong. Passions were set ablaze by this song, which reached Number One first in the UK and then in no fewer than 18 countries. And once they'd reached the point where all the world was, if not a stage, at least an audience,

● Boy George

○ CULTURE CLUB

there was no holding Culture Club back. The nature of the band's appeal was broad. The show they offered was not limited to a catchy tune: their music and lyrics reacted against the icy aloofness of new romantic pop and tugged unashamedly at the heartstrings; their colourful and varied clothing sent shockwaves through the fashion industry; they gave hope to millions of people of all ages to believe in themselves to express their feelings.

As soon as they caught the popular imagination it became clear that they were as much a social phenomenon as they were a pop group – their audience was *Coronation Street* as much as it was *Top Of The Pops.* They were outrageous, yet they were warm; they were stars, yet they were family. And if people were fascinated by Boy George's 'Gender Bender' image, they were at the same time reassured. He'd rather have a nice cup of tea than sex. Or would he?

Do You Really was followed by more successful hits. Their first album, **Kissing To Be Clever,** was a worldwide bestseller and they became the first band since the Beatles to have three singles from their debut album **(Do You Really, Time (Clock Of The Heart)** and **I'll Tumble 4 Ya)** reach the top ten in America's Billboard chart.

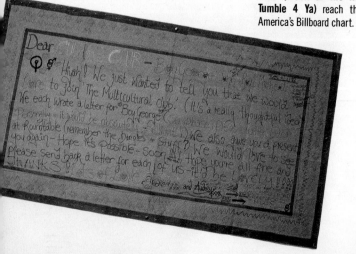

By the Autumn of 1983 their superstar status was unquestioned. **Karma Chameleon,** the first single to be released from their second album, **Colour By Numbers,** was an instant worldwide hit and when the band signed copies of their official biography *When Cameras Go Crazy* at a bookstore in North London, they nearly caused a riot: thousands of fans (including a fair number of mums) stampeded the ill-prepared shop. The band was forced to retreat to the cleaner's cupboard while security men reorganised the signing. *"By George! Boy Mania!"* observed the *Daily Star. "When fans go crazy"* commented the *Mail.*

With their second album, the band showed a remarkable musical range. George's own voice was admirably complemented by the redoubtable range of Helen Terry, who had already added a measure of manic soul to the between-albums single **Church Of The Poisoned Mind.**

The imagery also grew more complex and sophisticated for the second album. George had been on a well-publicised holiday to Egypt for two weeks before the release of **Karma Chameleon,** and, now working with Malcolm Garrett on packaging design, he created a distinctly

sphinx-like atmosphere for September '83. The album absorbed that feel and added further symbols, colours and, not surprisingly, numbers. In the album photographs (styled, of course, by George), the Boy looked young, vulnerable and innocent (who said things are rarely what they seem?), while Jon, Mikey and Roy looked fit, sporty and American.

Every time George went through customs, the headlines would pick up on his style. His basic 'look' was by now much more settled than in his pre-Culture Club nightclubbing days, when the only way you could be sure of recognising him was by picking out the most conspicuous object in the place. Now you could recognise his face and the general aspect of his hair, but one day he might be dressed in tartans, another in kaftan and turban, and a third (much to the dismay of French customs officials) as a Japanese geisha girl (*Show us you're a boy, George!" –Daily Mirror*).

Inevitably, Boy George has stolen much of the limelight as a media star. Indeed, it seems this is what he has prepared for all his life.

"I've got a very business-like attitude to publicity," he explains. *"I won't go out anywhere unless I want to be in the paper."* And if that sounds calculating, he points out it's only realistic. *"I know that if I go to a film première, for example, it'll be in the paper. And if I leave early, then it's going to say, 'Boy George left early, Boy George didn't like the film. So if I want to make a statement, then I make some kind of appearance — which is a visual statement."*

Being public property is a matter of give-and-take: *"I can't go out anywhere, I have no social life, I belong to the media. If I'm rude to a photographer or something they say, 'How dare you! We made you — you belong to the media.' So I think that if they're responsible for me, then they can give me some compensation — like the cover of The Sun."*

And for journalists, he is a godsend – not only because of his looks, but because he is quick-tempered, talkative (it's never easy to get a question in during an interview), self-contradicting, compassionate and always entertaining.

If at first he overshadowed the rest of the band to the extent that few people even knew who they were, the balance is now much more as they intended. Culture Club are a band of equals, in which each member makes his own contribution. That George includes image and publicity as part of his responsiblities is something the rest of the band accept.

"We always knew it was going to be like that," said Roy last year. "George has charisma and that sets him apart. He likes to talk — and he's better at it than the rest of us."

Commented Mikey: "It doesn't really worry me — business is straight behind all that. George is a good frontperson, that's his role in the band."

And Jon put it in perspective: "George has real talent. He could look normal, his dressing up is irrelevant. Of course, it's great and people love him, but above all it's his talent that shines through."

The other band members' own public profiles have developed particularly strongly over the last year and now, as often as not, radio and press interviews will be done by other members of the band, each of whom has built up a strong personal following.

Following their second album and extensive touring (part of which had to be rescheduled when Jon broke his finger), Culture Club devoted their energies to writing music and songs for the film *Electric Dreams*, and started work on their third album, **Waking Up With The House On Fire**. In doing so, they are opening up new areas in music and style and few will doubt that, more than any other pop band, they will continue to be an integral part of millions of homes, spreading across cultures and generations. Culture Club love their success, yet much of their appeal lies in the fact that they keep it in perspective.

"Ultimately," says George, "a relationship is more important to me, a love affair is more important than the success of Culture Club. You can't cross out emotion, you can't get rid of it. It will always be there in the shadows behind you, and I'm a very emotional person."

CULTURE CLUB ◯

JONATHAN AUBREY MOSS

Jonathan Aubrey Moss was born in London on September 11, 1957, and raised in a liberal Jewish environment. He became a promising schoolboy boxer, also developing his musical inclinations by practising regularly with his brother and Wang Chung's Nick Feldman, who lived across the street. After school he briefly joined his father in the rag trade before walking out, then he had a succession of jobs (as tape operator, cake salesman, apprentice printer, van driver and music agency assistant) before devoting himself entirely to music. Jon was the most experienced member of Culture Club when they started, having already played in a large number of bands, including Phone Bone Boulevard, Pastrami Barmy, Eskimo Norbert, The Clash, The Damned, The Edge and Adam And The Ants.

ROY HAY

Roy Ernest Hay was born in Southend on August 12, 1961, the second son in a docker's family. Until 1981, he lived at the family home in Corringham, close to Basildon, Essex. Discovering the guitar at 15, he became a 'guitar hero' for a while, learning all the solos and trying to beat every other guitarist in the area. Later he also developed an interest in piano and he started making some Joy Division-inspired tapes at home. Roy worked in a London insurance office for some three years after leaving school, followed by a stint as a hairdresser in Essex. In June, 1981, he met Alison Green, whom he was later to marry. Then, one day, his former insurance colleague Keith Giddons mentioned to George that he knew a good guitarist . . .

BOY GEORGE

George Alan O'Dowd was born at Bexley Hospital on June 14, 1961, the third son in an Irish Catholic family, with two younger brothers and a sister. For the first 12 years of his life, the family lived in a small, three-bedroom house in Joan Crescent, Eltham, South London, with all five boys sharing one bedroom, his sister Siobhan in another, his parents in the third and the two alsatians roaming more or less freely. In the seventies, he fell in love with Marc Bolan and Philadelphia Soul, started wearing outrageous clothes, drove his teachers beyond the edge of despair, got expelled from school and started making his presence felt in the nightclubs of London. By the end of the decade, after spending a year in Birmingham, he had become one of the nation's most prominent eccentrics.

MIKEY CRAIG

Michael Emile Craig was born in Hammersmith, London, on February 15, 1960. He has four sisters and two brothers. Mikey's father had been a singer in his native Jamaica before coming over to England to fight in the Second World War. In his first few years Mikey listened to a great deal of pop music (becoming an avid Monkees fan in the process). His parents made every effort to make him work at school and prepare for a good, solid profession, but he soon got bored at school and, at a tender age, started dancing and deejaying in Soho clubs. For several years he lived with a girlfriend, Cleo, and they had two children. His many efforts to put together a pop band bore fruit when he contacted George.

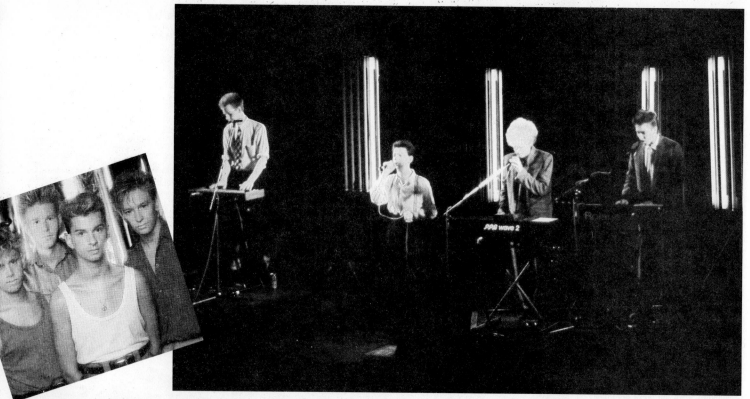

DEPECHE

● Above: Martin Gore, Andy Fletcher, David Gahan and Alan Wilder

Few bands nowadays are given the chance to change their colours midway through their career – yet Depeche Mode have made the transition from synth-poppers to agit-prop rockers with consummate ease and moreover, to much acclaim.

For too long the Basildon boy wonders were seen as nothing more then purveyors of an insipid score of bubble-gum pop tunes. It seemed that the most important thing they had to debate was how to pronounce their name. But with the release of their album, **Construction Time Again,** they unleashed on unsuspecting pop world a vibrant score of socialist lyrics and heavyweight rhythms. And suddenly they became the darlings of the press.

Depeche Mode's inception began in the early days of 1980, when three school friends, Vince Clarke, Martin Gore (born June 23, 1961) and Andy Fletcher (born July 9, 1961) played around with the bass, guitar and drums under the name of Composition Of Sound. Failing to make much progress on a conventional level, they decided to make moves towards the vogue for synthesisers. The New Romantics had just hit the clubs with their hearts on their sleeves and everything, everywhere, seemed geared toward the rising star of 'electro-pop'. The chips were down and the stakes were high. With the

addition of a gawky young chap called David Gahan (born June 9, 1962) and a quick change of name to Depeche Mode (literally 'hurried fashion') the new town wonders were in the running.

Their first gig was at The Bridgehouse and after a week's residency there, supporting Fad Gadget, they were spotted by a young DJ called Stevo. Stevo's addiction to the new futurist sound led him to release a compilation LP entitled **Some Bizarre,** which featured such (then) unknowns as Soft Cell, Blancmange and B-Movie. As luck would have it, Depeche Mode also found a slot. Their track **Photographic,** though still rough, was one of the best on the slate.

But their biggest break was meeting producer Daniel Miller, who had seen them at The Bridgehouse and was intent on signing them to his growing indie label, Mute Records. Their first release for Mute was **Dreaming Of Me** (February 1981), which scored a creditable top 60 placing, caught as it was on the first wave of synth-pop chart success. Their second single **New Life** catapaulted them to Number 11 and, with **Just Can't Get Enough,** their rise from small town creed to Big City Sound seemed complete. Yet, just as they were on their way, Vince Clarke, founder member and songwriter of all their material, upped and left. Purportedly because of his

DEPECHE MODE

handled the role with a capability far outstripping his age. His first single **See You** went to Number Six in the charts and was proof enough that the Mode could manage without their former songwriter.

Augmented by Vince's replacement, Alan Wilder (born June 1, 1959), the band toured America and the Orient, making noticeable inroads into the fierce Japanese market. At home, their young charm and schoolboyish looks kept them high in the charts with **Meaning Of Love, Leave In Silence** and their second LP, **Broken Frame.** But their angelic looks failed to find them favour with the press. Their fall from grace centred on their ability to seemingly float by, releasing an album here, a pop-ditty there. It was as if there was no real substance, as if they were nothing but a 'hurried fashion' after all – and one that had outstayed its welcome.

Fully aware of this fact, Martin Gore decided to let slip the facade of eternal youth and busied himself with writing a harder, more politically committed set for the third album **Construction Time Again.** The first augury of the band's new direction came with the powerful and accusatory tone of **Everything Counts,** which reached Number Six in the charts their biggest hit for a year and a half. The general nature of **Construction** was even harder hitting. The cover depicted a well built worker, sledge hammer in hand, looming large over a mountain top. Its themes of international socialism and world depression, married to a fine pop sensibility, caught the feelings of a nation and resulted in their best work to date.

As if this was not enough (the album went to Number Six), the follow up singles **Love In Itself** (lifted from the album) and **People Are People** both went top twenty (the latter reaching Number Four in March '84 – their highest placing so far).

As to whether they can capitalise on their success remains to be seen, but with **Construction Time Again** under their belts they're already walking down the right road.

feeling of restriction within the group, it was a sharp blow to the young and still inexperienced lads.

Vince, a particularly gifted musician (and a bit older than his erstwhile colleagues), wasted no time in making moves elsewhere and by the summer of 1982 he had formed a winning partnership with the big blues singer 'Alf' Moyet. Yazoo were a hit. With the demise of Yazoo in the summer of '83, Vince set up a new project with Eric Radcliffe and former Undertones man, Fergal Sharkey, called The Assembly.

Although Vince had written all but two of the tracks on their debut LP, **Speak And Spell,** the mantle of songwriter immediately fell upon Martin Gore, who

History may prove this judgement wrong, but May 8, 1984 was the day Duran Duran grew up. Grew up in the public eye and stopped being viewed just as performing mannequins for pubescent girls.

The Sun newspaper has never been renowned for the infallible accuracy of its claims. "*There are lies, damn lies and Sun Exclusives*" ran a famous leader in the *Daily Mirror*. But that day the front page excelled itself with "*Coke Crazy Duran Duran*" as a huge splash.

This was no reference to the soft drinks company who had just sponsored the Duran tour of the USA, but rather to their alleged fondness for cocaine. For three days *The Sun* titillated ten million readers with stories of the band's excesses back in '81 with drugs, girls and champagne — all spilled by an ex-minder, who had never actually been employed by them.

● John Taylor

It was no coincidence that these revelations coincided with Duran Duran's biggest ever hit in Britain, (or their refusal to do an interview with *The Sun*). **The Reflex** was Number One for a month. Accompanied by a stunning in-concert video, it quelled instantly those critics who felt compelled to compare the Birmingham quintet to a latter day Bay City Rollers.

Unwittingly *The Sun*, in a fit of pique, had given Duran Duran CREDIBILITY. It portrayed them as a rock band who worked hard and played hard; who were prey to the same temptations and excesses as the Rolling Stones or the Beatles. And it has always been the stated ambition of lead singer Simon Le Bon "*to be bigger than the Beatles or the Stones*".

Duran Duran have a long way to go to achieve that ambition. They probably never will, but they deserve the chance to be considered as contenders. Stop sniggering, they are good enough.

On April 5, 1984, Duran Duran played The Meadowlands, New Jersey. It is a hugh 22,000 seater hall just a few minutes over the polluted Hudson River from Manhattan island. The audience at the front of the auditorium is primarily teenage, at the back older.

Backstage, minutes before the band hits the stage, pandemonium reigns. The giant video screen will not be working; the girls will not be screaming every time a pretty face is flashed up on it. John Taylor — the recipient of most of those screams — shrugs his shoulders and says quietly: "*In that case we'll just have to see how good we really are.*"

And they do. At the back the fists of marijuana-smoking fathers are pounding the air alongside those of their pre-teen daughters. The version of **Planet Earth** with which Duran close their show is very different from the one they did on *Top Of The Pops* way back in February 1981. But then they are very different people now.

Nowadays all five Durans will cringe with embarrassment at the sight of such early pictures. Only drummer Roger Taylor so much as looks the same: guitarist Andy Taylor was a platinum blond in grey leather trousers; Nick Rhodes was a precocious 19-year-old with strawberry blond hair in a costume that would have split Beau Brummell's sides; John Taylor hid behind frills and thick pancake; while Simon Le Bon, without his streaks, resembled nothing more than an over-weight gay caballero.

Those were the early days of the New Romantics, when pop stars were running riot in the kiddies' dressing up box. (Spandau Ballet were clad in kilts and medieval jerkins). For Duran Duran this was their first and perhaps only 15 minutes of fame. They were earning £50 a week and determined to enjoy it while it lasted.

Fifty quid a week was more than John and Nick had ever envisaged back at the beginning, the day they sat in a Birmingham pub and talked about names. It could have been RAF until the film *Barbarella* came into the conversation and they remembered a baddie called Duran Duran.

Nicholas James Bates (he plucked the Rhodes from his favourite piano, because legend has it that he objected to his schoolboy nickname "Master Bates") was born in Birmingham on June 8, 1962. By 16 he had abandoned school as a dead loss and formed a punk band with a black haired, spotty bespectacled youth called Nigel.

Nigel John Taylor (born June 20, 1962) is now better known inside the band as JT. At the time he was at art school, having failed a bunch of A Levels, and tested his art teachers by producing nothing more than the first Duran Duran demonstration tape for his final year presentation. His tutors failed to recognise the potential of a song called **Girls on Film.**

Early Durannies came and went with the waxing and waning of the moon — including Steve Duffy (aka TinTin), who is now signed to WEA Records. Depressed with the lack of potential in Nick's rhythm box, they recruited drummer Roger Andrew Taylor (born April 26, 1960 in Castle Bromwich).

Roger's musical career had first been awakened at the age of ten by the Jackson Five. He graduated through Genesis into punk by being able to hit *"as many drums as possible in a tenth of a second".*

When John switched from playing lead to bass guitar after *"really listening to Bernard Edwards, the bass player in Chic"*, Duran set about refining an individual sound. To their earlier Roxy Music/David Bowie influences, they added a funky American feel.

Next onto the scene were the Berrow brothers – Paul and Michael. Impressed by the glitter and style they had seen on rent in New York's Studio 54 discoteque they determined to recreate the decadent ambience in their Birmingham night-club, the Rum Runner.

Duran Duran needed some place to perform so Nick and John walked into the club one day with the tape JT had presented to his art school tutors. The Berrows, according to Roger, *"were looking for a band that was a cross between Gino Soccio, Genesis and Chic."*

But what Duran Duran were still missing was the guitarist and the singer of their dreams. The last two to join the band were also the two furthest removed in both class and personality; Andy Taylor and Simon Le Bon.

Andy (born February 16th, 1961) was born and brought up in a tiny fishing village, Cullercoates, near Newcastle-upon-Tyne. The family had an outside toilet, a tin bath and no money. Which perhaps helps to account for Andy's penchant for flaunting his newly acquired wealth and enjoying the excesses of rock stardom to the very full.

After a stint playing in a pop group in Germany, Andy spotted an ad for a guitarist for this Brummie group, and hopped on a train down. John and Roger were convinced by his musical ability, Nick by his mouth. All three forgot to tell him they did not actually have a singer.

● **Simon Le Bon**

Simon John Charles le Bon (born October 27th, 1958 in Bushey, Hertfordshire) is the eldest of three sons in a family descended from the Huguenots – French Protestants who escaped religious persecution in the 17th Century. From the age of five his mother was determined he should live up to the star quality of his name and enrolled him in acting classes. The local choirmaster in Pinner parish church convinced him to sing.

In 1979 he was studying drama at Birmingham University, his ex-girlfriend worked as a barmaid at the Rum Runner. He turned up to audition for Duran Duran in pink spotted leopard skin trousers. He was impressed by their commitment and professionalism – something that has always been Duran's major asset.

Simon quit college in the summer of 1980. Michael Berrow sold his house to finance Duran's support spot on the Hazel O'Connor tour. They were sleeping in a camper van and earning £10 a week each. But by the end of the tour, as Hazel's manager recalls, *"They were drawing their own crowd"* and they had a record contract with EMI.

In retrospect, Duran Duran were fortunate in their timing. They were not punks and so were allowed to develop a personality and a musical style away from the watchful eyes of the mass media. So that when they were finally "discovered" in November 1982, thousands of fans already knew that they were the biggest band in Britain.

Screaming teenagers mobbing pretty boys at airports had been out of fashion for ten years. In the aftermath of 1977 pop music was a symbol of outrage, of literally spitting at authority. Johnny Rotten was a style and a pose, but it was impossible to dance and pick up girls while he screeched through **Anarchy In The UK,** Duran Duran brought chic back to the public eye – both stylistically and musically.

But because they were always honest about their intentions and ambitions – success in financial terms as well as public recognition – the serious critics hated them for not hiding the prostitution of their art.

However, the little girls understood and they did not care. The five hunks in Duran Duran were their secret, one that did not have to be shared with adults or elder brothers.

DURAN

"We knew we had stumbled onto something on our first headlining tour in '81," recalls John Taylor, "I think it was in Brighton, but we were behind the curtain and all I could hear were these girls screaming. It was eerie."

Eerie or not, hit single followed hit single. The rise of Duran closely mirrors that of the glossy pop fortnightly *Smash Hits*. Both appealed to the teen market and offered no more and no less than they promised.

The first eponymous Duran Duran album yielded three hit singles. **Planet Earth** led to **Careless Memories** and

then into **Girls on Film.** Right from the time **Planet Earth** first touched down in the charts, its profits were ploughed straight back into the band, whether it was touring, or making videos.

Duran Duran were the first rock band to properly exploit the video technology. Previously the clips had enhanced, even made one single into a one-off hit. Duran used video to enhance their image immeasurably.

By filming with top video director, Australian Russell Mulcahy, in such supposedly "exotic" locations as Sri Lanka and Antigua, Duran promoted themselves into the fantasy world of the jet set. Their fans hardly objected at the sight of a few tanned torsos.

It also freed the boys to concentrate on

taking their message to the people of the world, secure in the knowledge that everywhere they went the videos had been before and would be again after they left. 1982's **Rio** album spawned four Top Ten Hits in the UK; **My Own Way, Hungry Like The Wolf, Save A Prayer** and **Rio** itself.

Most important of all, it was video that broke Duran in the USA. A couple of tours, including a spot supporting Blondie in football stadiums, did nothing to excite the kids in America. Then Music Tele Vision happened – a 24 hour cable TV service that broadcast nothing but pop videos and more pop videos.

When MTV broadcast a Duran special on New Year's Eve '82, it did more to break the band than seven months of touring had. Their American record company, Capitol, had despaired of **Rio** breaking into the Top Fifty. Thanks to

Simon Le Bon
Vocals
"We combined really hard work with careful planning, because you can slog your guts out and get nowhere, just playing tatty little clubs. We're shrewd. You have to be to get any distance."

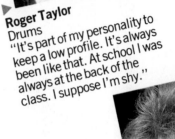

Roger Taylor
Drums
"It's part of my personality to keep a low profile. It's always been like that. At school I was always at the back of the class. I suppose I'm shy."

Andy Taylor
Guitar
"I suppose it is fabulous, going to all these countries and having instant acceptance. It's very hit and miss though, It could be over tomorrow."

Nick Rhodes
Keyboards
"One of the major reasons for our band's success is that we don't have times when somebody really loses control of reality. You've just got to keep a karma throughout."

John Taylor
Guitar
"I think we've made something out of nothing pretty quickly; we haven't had it all laid on a plate regardless of what some people say."

MTV and the band's own foresight, within a year they had had three Duran Duran albums in the US Top Ten.

Meanwhile in Britain, Japan and Australia – the first country to recognise their universal appeal – the order of the day was Duran Mania. In the UK their arrival at the top was confirmed at the Radio One/Daily Mirror Rock and Pop Awards in February 1983. They scooped the Best Band Award, winning more votes than the next five groups put together.

What should have been their crowning glory was an invitation to appear at a charity concert before Prince Charles and Princess Diana. Hundreds of fans greeted them at Heathrow airport and media overkill was the order of the day. The actual concert was a disaster, both technically and aesthetically, despite a Number One single in **Is There Something I Should Know?**. At least they were all men enough to admit the show was a fiasco.

By now the video image had become a

reality. They were all jet set playboys. Andy Taylor had married Tracey Wilson, his hairdresser girlfriend, a year previously, but when Simon le Bon announced his engagement to Canadian model Clare Stansfield, it was front page news. (A year later the romance quietly ended.) Within a year JT was threatening to wed topless model Janine Andrews and Nick Rhodes was affianced to American heiress Julie Ann Friedman. Roger just kept quiet about his long-term romance with dancer Giovanna Cantone.

What they could not drop was the teeny bop tag. Their third album **Seven And The Ragged Tiger** – the fruits of seven months of labour in recording studios in the Caribbean and Australia – was more adventurous, musically.

The album's first two hits, **Union Of The Snake** and **New Moon On Monday** failed to impress by the high standards Duran Duran had set themselves. The British media had found a new pop toy to play with – Boy George. The rise of Culture Club has been even more meteoric and even more successful. Unsurprisingly there is little love lost between the two outfits.

There is something universally appealing about Culture Club's music – as if they were the natural heirs to the Beatles. Whereas around Duran Duran there is an air of deliberation and calculation – The Rolling Stones without the natural outrage.

The Sun, in its self-appointed role as guardian of the country's morals, drove home the Stones analogy. *The Daily Mirror,* with an uncharacteristically tacky buy-up of the memoirs of an ex-girlfriend of John Taylor's, confirmed it. The teenage girls who read the articles just refused to believe them.

Whatever the girls' older relations thought, lots of them went out and bought **The Reflex** – produced by the band's long time hero Nile Rodgers, the guitarist from Chic.

It has always been Duran Duran's intention to fuse the British rock theatre traditions of Roxy Music and David Bowie with the American disco dance floor sensibilities of Chic.

Having done that they no longer have the need to dress up in Antony Price suits, or film exhilarating travelogues on tropical islands. Unless they want to.

Duran Duran have achieved the second most difficult task in rock and roll music. They have climbed the slippery ladder to the topmost point. For Simon le Bon to achieve his much stated ambition they have to tackle the most difficult task in rock and roll – to stay at the top for the next ten years.

EURYTH

Tourists' direction – Peet Coombes was, after all, the main songwriter. But, spurred by the adverse criticism, they wanted to become more adventurous and several vicious fights broke out between Annie and Peet, with a bewildered Dave caught in the middle. Eventually, while on tour in Bangkok, they all agreed the best thing was to quit, and there was an overwhelming sigh of relief from all concerned.

Though the effect of the Tourists split was still shattering, Dave and Annie wasted no time in launching a new project, accompanied by an ambitious manifesto.

"Eurythmics is not a band in a conventional sense. Instead it will be a partnership, a nucleus of Annie and I, around which we'll work with a variety of musicians, subject to availability and compatibility," decreed Dave.

It took them several years to put these bold words into practice and it wasn't really surprising that they couldn't live up to these early boasts – they were still trying to live down the ghost of the Tourists!

They were an odd couple right from the start.

Annie recalls *"The first thing he said was 'Will you marry me?' I thought he was a serious nutter — and I was right, he did look ... a bit strange."*

The meeting of Annie Lennox (who was a waitress at the time) and Dave Stewart (who was a mess) was a momentous occasion.

Annie vividly remembers *"For me it was love at first sight, although all he wanted to do was talk about music. We immediately moved into a new flat and lived together for the next six years.*

"It didn't take much for him to persuade me to give up waitressing and a few days later we marched into a record company office playing acoustic guitars. They offered us a deal on the spot and we accepted as we were completely broke and needed the cash."

The result of this miraculous event was teaming up with a guitarist called Peet Combes to release a single under the collective name of The Catch. It seemed like the sort of overnight success story you read about in glossy magazines.

And then, suddenly ... nothing! The single flopped and Logo records obviously didn't view The Catch as a long-term prospect, despite agreeing that they had some excellent songs. Aware that they really needed a proper band to play live concerts, the trio of Dave, Annie and Peet recruited a drummer and bassist and – discarding an initial group name of the Spheres Of

Celestial Influence – the Tourists were born!

In the middle of 1977's punk uniformity of earnest outrage, the Tourists were a splash of colour in a dull grey landscape and their bright, bouncy, jangly melodicism soon made them immensely popular, even if it was occasionally too superficial or redolent of the sixties pop culture.

Singles like **Blind Among the Flowers** and **The Loneliest Man In The World** soon established them as a recognised chart act, but when they innocently released a spirited version of Dusty Springfield's **I Only Wanna Be With You,** it was as though the whole world went mad!

It dashed up the charts to Number Four and the public took the Tourists to their heart, especially the blonde bombshell in dayglo earrings, Annie Lennox. But the music press seemed incensed and dismissed the band as mere sixties copyists and dubbed Annie 'difficult' and 'icy'.

Virtually at the height of their career, this criticism was like a mortal wound and by the time they arrived in Montserrat to record their third album, the cracks were beginning to show.

At this time, Dave and Annie weren't particularly active in shaping the

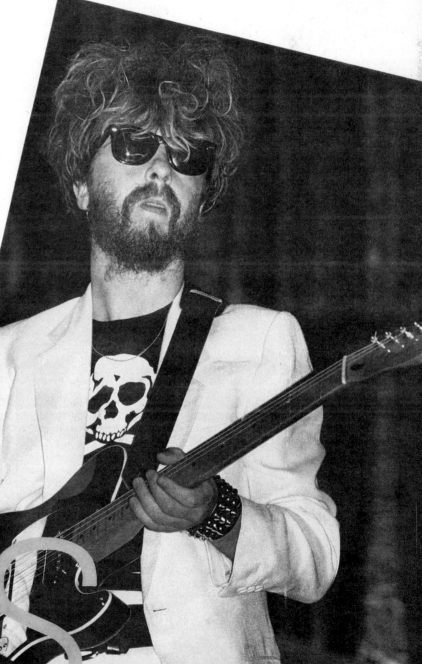

EURYTHMICS

Annie especially felt she had to start a new career, a new life. *"The image of Annie Lennox of the Tourists was so strong and easy to pick out — I just want people to realist I'm not this nice, popsy, happy-go-lucky Annie, who I DETEST! So I decided to kill her, dead."*

Their debut album **In The Garden** was a step forward, but lacked proper direction. Recorded in Germany with Conny Planck — who incidentally had produced the first Tourists album as well — it hinted at a muted soul influence, mixed in with more traditional folk ideas, but overall it was an unsuccessful (though intriguing) experiment.

Dave Stewart later referred to it as *"a change-over phase from the Tourists — we were just messing around almost, trying to capture a certain feeling."*

And to an extent, it worked — but really if Eurythmics were to be a successful project, they had to exert even more control over their destiny. So far they'd travelled abroad to record an album produced by someone else, which sounded like it contained more of other people's ideas than their own, and they hadn't yet found a strong image with which to present this new concept.

Then two coincidental events occurred which were to change the course of Eurythmics' career.

First Annie Lennox cut her hair and stopped wearing wigs. And then — having found the perfect image (clean, sharp, slightly sophisticated) — they found the perfect music: electronic soul.

"I'd always been drawn to soul music" explained Annie. *"I used to dance to early Motown like Stevie Wonder, early Supremes and Marvin Gaye when I was a kid in Aberdeen.*

"In Eurythmics, we've tried to take some of the energy from punk, the sweetness from soul music and the alienation of European synthetic mechanical rhythms — and tried to blend it all together."

In late 1982, their new single **Love Is A Stranger** began to make waves. It had mystique, an irrepressible dance beat, a hint of sexual menace and a heart-stopping fabulous vocal.

At last Annie was realising the vast potential of that voice and soon critics and public alike were seduced. She was compared to Dusty Springfield and called *"the best white voice around".*

And then **Sweet Dreams** cracked open the charts and Eurythmics were catapulted from virtual oblivion to the giddy heights of international acclaim.

From having no recognisable image to being the face of the eighties, Annie Lennox stared out of every poster, record sleeve and magazine cover, while Dave Stewart got on with the business of producing the **Sweet Dreams** album, recorded in a tiny eight-track studio above a factory in London's Camden Town.

Featuring deeply touching, emotional songs like **Jennifer** and **This City Never Sleeps,** as well as the two hit singles, the album was an instant smash, as was the British tour that coincided with its release.

Dave and Annie were having their cake and eating it — and then came the delightful, mesmerising videos, the proverbial icing on the cake.

The self-scripted storylines were fast-moving and captivating, and Annie looked cool and aloof, becoming a new sex symbol by playing with traditional female roles. While her love of disguises and acting had once hindered Eurythmics' progress by confusing the public, it was now this very same confusion and changing public image that had everyone talking about them! Suddenly it was like Eurythmics had been released from a life sentence of purgatory and were on permanent holiday. Like children let loose in a toy factory, they couldn't resist trying everything — and it all seemed to turn to gold!

Staying true to their concept of Eurythmics as a project rather than a band, they formed loose liasons with a variety of performers, including avant-garde musicians such as Holger Czukay, Robert Crash and Jackie Leibzeit, as well as pop stars like Clem Burke from Blondie, Scritti Politti's Green Gartside, the Associates' Billy Mackenzie and female vocalist Kiki Dee.

Just when it seemed this diversity had become as extreme as was possible, they released a new single called **Who's That Girl**, which zoomed into the top five and then proceeded to make a video which featured a cast that read like *Who's Who In Eighties Female Pop* ... Cheryl and Jay from Buck's Fizz, Kate from Haysi Fantayzee, Kiki Dee, Sarah, Keren and Siobhan from Bananarama, Hazel O'Connor and – the crowning glory – a then-unknown Marilyn!

And the video itself caused a sensation! Playing up to the public's curiosity about Annie's sexuality, they arranged a clever dramatic/technical device, whereby Annie was pictured in the final shot in a passionate embrace – with an image of herself as a man!

"I just thought I'd take it to extremes" she laughed. *"Dressing up as a man wasn't enough — I had to be a man!"*

With barely a pause to tour America and Europe, Eurythmics consolidated their position as leading innovators with the **Touch** album, a cool, sensuous blend of raucous soul power and seductive, soothing synthesisers.

Songs like **Here Comes The Rain Again** and **No Fear, No Hate, No Pain** became instant favourites, mixing heartache with technology.

"I find electronics very passionate" explained Annie. *"Synthesisers are only cold when used in a clichéd way."*

When put like that, the Eurythmics story all makes sense, as though it were almost inevitable. But in fact, Eurythmics are one of the most unlikely partnerships imaginable. Annie Lennox is a quiet, precise, highly personable and private woman from Scotland (born Christmas Day, 1954) – brought up an only child whose best friend was often her own imagination.

Dave Stewart is a spontaneous, scruffy, scatterbrained wizard from Sunderland, who benefitted from a somewhat unorthodox upbringing in a fairly musical family. Born September 9, 1952, he ran away from home at the age of 16 and has been playing music ever since.

Eurythmics really is like a jigsaw. They're an odd couple who happen to fit together – and it's this unlikely attraction of opposites that is central to their very success.

"Yeah, we're total opposites" agrees Annie. *"Dave's a complete optimist, well-balanced and undaunted by anything, whereas I'm a depressive pessimist!"*

"And we work completely differently too" adds Dave. *"I work amazingly quickly, whereas Annie is much more selective — she'll spend two weeks on just four lines of lyrics, whereas I tend to have 12 backing tracks and bits of melodies all over the place.*

"But that's our different personalities — my flat is like that, stuff all over the floor and tapes hanging out of cupboards, but Annie's flat is very kind of precise.

"But that works well — if we were both

like me, we'd probably have about a thousand unfinished songs, and if we were both like Annie, we'd probably have just one single every two years!))

"Annie and I love that sort of duality," Dave continued. *"It's the subject of nearly every song we've written, from* **Love Is A Stranger** *to* **Who's That Girl**. *It's the duality of EVERYTHING — the tramp lying on the street, while somebody walks by in a fur coat, the feeling of love mixed up with terrible feelings of guilt and remorse — the whole of life is that sort of constant turmoil. It's great, it's terrible — that's the way it is!"*

And that's the way it is all over the world, which is where Eurythmics were in 1984 – Japan, Australia, France, America, on holiday in Africa ... everywhere except Britain!

But what of the future – it's something no one can accurately predict (who would have even dared suggest their current success two years ago?), but that doesn't stop everyone having an opinion.

As with any successful group, Eurythmics have had to face an occasionally intrusive and malicious press – rumours about Annie quitting were printed almost daily at one time, and of course that's always a possibility, which she herself had admitted. In fact, the interview that sparked off one such rumour (in *Record Mirror*) was no more than an admission of that possibility, and certainly not a statement of intent.

And the newly-married Annie? Perhaps a family, perhaps a film career?

"We are finishing off years of work now — Dave and I haven't stopped working for six years and we've worked really, really hard every day."

"There has to come a time when you say No Eurythmics, No Annie Lennox, No Dave Stewart, No Nothing — just disappear — and that's going to come very soon."

It's fairly obvious Annie was there referring to a rest, but not retirement – though a certain disreputable daily paper chose to interpret it differently as their headline of *"Annie says she'll give up rock"* suggests. They could have easily – and truthfully – written *"Dave Stewart admits he's going to die",* since both events will inevitably happen at some time in the future, but exactly when is just pure speculation.

What has to be remembered about Annie Lennox is that she is a very disciplined and ambitious performer, who studied classical piano and flute at the Royal College of Music when she was 17. Both she and Dave have struggled too long and hard to give it all up overnight.

But there are many alternatives.

Jack Steven, who guided their career when he was in Artist Development at RCA Records reckons Dave's future career will be as a record producer – *"I'm sure that's where his real talent lies",* while Chris Ashbrook, who was the lighting cameraman on nearly all of Eurythmics

videos, rates Annie as one of the most natural performers he's ever worked with.

For their own part, Dave says *"If Eurythmics finished tomorrow, I'd get a mobile studio and travel round the world recording for my limited edition label!"*

When after a whirlwind romance, Annie married German Hare Krishna devotee Rhada Raman in April '84, the music business rocked to rumours that she was about to retire into a religious life. Such myths are mere ill informed speculation.

"I hope being married will give me the kind of stability and love everybody wants and needs," says Annie.

"Rhada is a very good influence to have around. He's a very special person who has given me a great deal of support and stability.

"I want my livelihood and what I like doing to be the same thing — and I'm lucky that I'm doing that right now. I've no desire to be a solo artist at all. I cannot imagine not working with Dave."

In love as in all things Annie Lennox has always been her own woman, just as musically Eurythmics have always tried to forge their own way. And will continue to do so.

● Frankie goes bespectacled: Brian Nash, Ped Gill, Holly Johnson and Mark O'Toole. Paul Rutherford preferred to stay in bed that day…

Outrage has always played a massive – and underrated – role in the marketing of rock and roll music. How else could Bill Haley – visually an overweight red neck dressed in a dinner jacket – have shocked a nation with a song that simply suggested dancing the night away.

How else could a bunch of scruffy kids in love with playing Rhythm and Blues, but incapable of writing their own material, have metamorphosed into that mid-sixties nightmare of all respectable parents, the Rolling Stones?

Or what about that bunch of yobs whose clothes were all held together by safety pins, who had short spiky hair rather than that trendy long stuff? They went on telly, were being asked perfectly sensible questions by that nice Bill Grundy and they replied using rude four letter words beginning with F. Remember the Sex Pistols?

It happened again in 1984. In January, the perfect month to confirm paranoids that there was still a chance for Orwell to be right after all.

There was this jolly ordinary pop song **Relax** cruising it's way up the charts. (Actually it was not that ordinary, but more of that later). Then one Wednesday morning Radio One disc jockey Mike Read decreed that the said **Relax** had absolutely the opposite effect on him, that it was disgusting and all about sex. (Pop music, of course, has never been about sex!)

Decreeing that this filthy record would never be heard again on *his* radio show, Read hurtled it across the studio, where presumably it shattered into two million pieces. Breakfast in thousands of households was momentarily interrupted before the population got back to ordinary life and went off to work or

school.

And that's where it should all have ended. Read would have been forgiven his tantrum and Frankie Goes To Hollywood might still have gone to Number One. For to give **Relax** full credit, it is a totally brilliant dance record, coupling a stirring chorus with a rippling rhythm that drags weary feet war whooping across the floor. It is not so much a record about everyday boy-meets-girl, they kiss-and-cuddle-a-bit sex, but about a nuclear session between the sheets. Exhilarating, but exhausting.

The problem was that the two singers admitted that they were homosexuals. They were also signed to a brand new record label owned by their producer Trevor Horn, Zang Tuum Tuub (reputedly that is the sound made when you thump a drum). And ZTT's marketing was in the hands of the fiendish Paul Morley.

FRANKIE GOES

Readers of *The New Musical Express* know of Morley as a fairly vicious, intense, Mancunian writer, suffering from a love-hate relationship with the music business. Morley had come out of punk and he was determined to recreate, artificially if necessary, the outrage of that era.

Frankie Goes To Hollywood were the perfect vehicle, ready made to clone into OUTRAGE. **Relax's** sleeve is deliberately sexually ambiguous. The first 12 inch mix was provocatively called a "Sex Mix", the sleeve notes threatened and tantalised. But the *coup de grâce* can be found in one corner of the seven inch single sleeve.

Printing lyrics is not an original ploy, but here for children of all ages to see were the immortal lines: *"Relax don't do it when you want to suck it to it, relax don't do it when you want to come."*

The suggestion of fellatio was too much for the BBC. Most of the bosses went to public school, so to their minds the implication was obvious. The song was all about two men having sex together.

So Read's ban metamorphosed into a fullscale corporation wipe out. It was slightly embarassing that Radio One had played **Relax** some 90 times previously and that Frankie had done one *Top Of The Pops* already. The controversy caused by the ban, fuelled by Fleet Street (which for once did not agree with the Beeb and don its role as moral arbiter of the country), shot the record to the top of the charts.

"The whole **Relax** *thing was ridiculous,"* says second singer Paul Rutherford, *"I do not condone what Mike Read did censoring it. He does not have the right. Maybe he thinks he does, sitting there with his headphones on.*

"We hold no malice towards him. If anything we can thank him for making it a more important record than it was. But I'm not going to."

It was poetic justice that Read was the DJ with the honour of introducing Frankie on *Top Of The Pops* the week their second single **Two Tribes** began its chart career at the very top.

Meanwhile, **Relax** had started to go up the charts again, attaining a life and behaviour pattern unique even in the rock world.

At the very moment when Frankie Goes To Hollywood should have been heard in every home in the land 12 times a day ad nauseam, there was nothing. Just silence. Everyone wanted to hear Frankie, to see Frankie, to touch Frankie and they were not allowed to. The record buying public is like a child: what it cannot have, it must have.

After releasing just two singles, Frankie Goes To Hollywood have become one of the country's major rock bands. And still no one knows much about them. Except, perhaps, that they are all from Liverpool and are intent on breaking one of that city's fabled pop records. Only Gerry and the Pacemakers had Number Ones with all their first three releases.

William "Holly" Johnson was born in 1960 in Wavertree, not far from Penny Lane. (In the early days he used to claim to being born in Khartoum in the Sudan). His father worked first as a seaman, then as an insurance salesman, then as a building worker.

Liverpool has – because of the docks – always enjoyed a more carefree night life, been more open to the bizarre and the foreign, but as a teenager young William still managed to shock the neighbourhood.

"I used to shave me head and paint it red and green. People wrote to the Liverpool Echo saying 'Who's this Martian walking around town?"

Hanging out in a club for *"15-year-old weirdos"* he bumped into Paul Rutherford (born 1959 in Liverpool, with a merchant seaman father). They have been friends ever since.

"Decadence was the key word then. We were all into a bisexual scene. The name Holly was given to me by a girl called Yvonne Petrovitch, because of the Andy Warhol connection with the transvestite Holly Woodlawn."

Holly's first musical gig was in local outfit Big In Japan, playing guitar behind singer Jayne Casey. At the time Paul Rutherford was sharing a flat with Pete Burns, the singer in Dead Or Alive.

"We started off as local weirdos getting into fights and ended up as landmarks. We used to congregate at Eric's."

Eric's, built on the site where the Cavern Club had once housed lunchtime gigs from the Beatles, was the seminal Liverpool club. It was there that Echo and the Bunnymen, Julian Cope (Teardrop Explodes), Orchestral Manoeuvres In The Dark, Wah and other bands with silly names and interesting ideas, congregated and began to expand.

They will probably try to deny it, but the three musicians in Frankie were too young to really become part of the Eric's scene. They were still at school – or not, as the case may be.

Peter Gill – better known as Ped – was born in 1964, near the Aintree racecourse. He was given a drum kit for his 16th birthday, eight months later he formed Dancing Girl with guitarist Brian 'Nasher' Nash (born in May 1963) and bass man Mark O'Toole (born January '64), Nasher's cousin.

By their own admission it was not an earth shattering outfit. Ped left and

picked up with Holly in Sons Of Egypt. Searching for a guitarist, they were joined by Mark's brother Jed – who later quit because he had a wife, a kid, a job and a house. It became Frankie Goes To Hollywood.

Holly pinched the name from a poster he once saw advertising a Frank Sinatra tour. From the outset the intention was to be different.

"I had just seen Annabella Lwin from Bow Wow Wow," says Holly, *"It was pure sex on legs. I thought we might be able to cause some similar reaction. Our idea was to seduce everyone into a life of pure pleasure."*

and a black leather peaked cap. It was aggressively macho and obviously gay. Even then Frankie had the aura of the Sex Pistols. They were dangerous.

Even without the added Morley touch, the early Frankie shows were outrageous. Originally they had a girl singer and a couple of Leather Pettes clad in black and chained to pillars. Paul – back from a sojourn in London – saw a gig one night. It excited him so much he leapt up on the stage and has stayed there ever since.

Early videos of the band have Paul wearing a pair of backless leather chaps,

It was Channel Four's Newcastle based rock show that provided the next piece of the jigsaw. Unsigned, with record companies sniffing around them, but basically incapable of marketing the heavy sexual image, Frankie wowed the TV audience on The Tube. They also impressed Paul Morley. He convinced Trevor Horn, who had simultaneously heard a Frankie demo on Richard Skinner's Radio One show.

Trevor Horn is a shy bespectacled chap, who is now regarded as the most exhilarating record producer in the known universe. Beginning his career as singer in Buggles – remember the insidious, **Video Killed The Radio Star?** – he graduated into an incarnation of the ponderous seventies supergroup Yes, before finding his real niche behind the control board. Productions for ABC **(Lexicon Of Love)**, Dollar, Yes (he even gave them a US Number One with **Owner Of A Lonely Heart**) and Malcolm McLaren's series of ethnic musical guerilla raids **(Duck Rock)**, have resulted in a full cheque book, critical acclaim and Frankie Goes To Hollywood.

Speculation about whether Frankie can survive without Trevor's over the top, Armageddon approach to production or Morley's blatant media manipulation are

currently irrelevant. **Two Tribes** is not as great a song as **Relax,** but the finished product is far more powerful.

It may be noised about as the *"first genuine protest song of the eighties"* – a totally ridiculous assumption – but it is a straightforward indictment of super-power politics. Holly did write it during the Falklands War and the accompanying video is quite simply chilling.

The sight of Reagan and Chernenko gouging, pummeling, kneeing each other in the groin and biting each other's ear is very brutal, but it is not mindless. The globe exploding at the end is a cliché, but it works. It might even be considered educational.

The real test for Frankie Goes To Hollywood will come in 1985. There is a limit to the amount of hype even Paul Morley can inflict on a gullible public. **Two Tribes** took three months to make and their debut album has to come out this autumn.

Welcome To The Pleasure Dome – its title tantalisingly gay, but actually lifted from Samuel Taylor Coleridge's opium inspired epic poem – will prove whether all Frankie's songs (lyrics by Holly, music by Mark and Ped) can live to their early promise. Then will come the second test, the concert stage.

Live Frankie are fundamentally a guitar, bass and drums trio. They will have to stand alone, without the Trevor Horn mega-mix, without the videos. But they are not worried unduly.

"We want to create an aura of controversy," says Mark O'Toole, *"Because we set out to do something different.*

"We are at the top and we aim to stay there. Just look at that poof in a dress and make up, Boy George; he's dying now. Spandau Ballet have been doing the same thing for the last three years, soppy ballads.

"Duran Duran might survive on being musicians, but not because they're pretty faces. And don't mention Wham! in the same breath as us."

Dismissing the opposition with words is easy enough. But the five Frankies have surrounded themselves with that Liverpudlian scally (slang for scalliwag) arrogance that once characterised the Fab Four. They have coupled that with the breath of scandal that catapulted the Stones into prominence.

Back in the sixties no one wanted their daughter to marry a Stone. In the eighties they probably wouldn't mind their daughter sleeping with a Frankie. But as for their son . . .

"Lock up your sons and daughters. Frankie is coming to town," Holly used to say in his early interviews, unaware of the fascination the heterosexual has for the homosexual lifestyle. *"You should see some of the pictures we've had taken.*

We're going to have to buy back all the negatives."

Holly and Paul have learnt their lesson now.

"At the beginning Holly and I were very honest and totally naive," admits Paul. "I'm glad I'm gay, I'm glad I came clean about it, but we're not waving any banners. Frankie only waves the banner of having fun.

"With **Relax** we showed how obssessed and prejudiced people are about sex. Anyone accusing us of perpetrating the gay stereotype is talking through their arse.

"I'm bored with it. There are a million and one faggots you can interview about being gay.

"We are entertainers. For want of a better word."

Holly has one: "My favourite thing is singing. Singing is better than sex."

Likewise, if Frankie does actually get to Hollywood, likes it and stays there, Holly Johnson might be the superstar for the 21st century. Thereby proving the old adage that nothing succeeds like excess.

● The striking *Two Tribes* video

HEAVEN 17

Pop history is littered with tales of working class boys made good, and this tale is no different. Our story begins in Sheffield, until recently not exactly a hot-bed of pop music talent, but Heaven 17 have been one of the groups to change all that.

Singer Glenn Gregory remembers growing up in a decaying industrial landscape — times were hard: "Things like back-to-back houses, outside toilets and no bathroom. My Mum, Dad, brother and I all shared the same bedroom until I was eight. It's embarrassing to talk about it now, because people think you're exaggerating."

It's all a far cry from the hi-tech — company exec. image portrayed by Heaven 17 some years later, but as you work through the material from their LPs, you'll find constant references to the environment from which they sprung. The single, **Crushed By The Wheels Of Industry,** is one such example, a state of affairs the trio were at pains to avoid.

"My Dad's fantasy was to have an office job because he was on his feet all day working as a tool grinder." Martyn Ware decided he wanted something different.

The early signs weren't good as Ware, Ian Craig-Marsh and Glenn Gregory moved through a succession of factory and supermarket jobs. But they hadn't given up all hope of escaping the treadmill.

The three finally met at an arts/theatre workshop called The Meatwhistle, and this proved to be the catalyst needed to launch the trio towards the lifestyle they so desperately craved.

The corporate suit and tie which has been so central to Heaven 17's image building may have helped to intimidate music biz types, but that well-heeled look belies their first appearances at The Meatwhistle in the early seventies.

"I remember when Ian first walked into the workshop. He looked absolutely weird, was totally unreliable and had just been kicked out of school for being a subversive element," Glenn said later.

"Mind you, Martyn looked just as absurd. He used to go down to The Meatwhistle wearing white flares and silver platform boots with five inch heels!

"It has to be said that glam rock was at its height and I wasn't exactly well dressed in my 24 inch flared jeans and gold baseball boots either."

It wasn't long before Ian and Glenn formed a group with the dubious title of Musical Vomit! All in all it was a bit of a non-starter – the highlight of the band's short lived career was getting pelted with cans thrown by irate hippies at the Bath Festival!

As the seventies wore on, more and more groups sprang up in Sheffield, and it was these enthusiasts who were later to form groups like Cabaret Voltaire, Clock DVA and the Human League.

Craig-Marsh and Ware in the meantime had abandoned their shop floor jobs for more stimulating careers as computer operators, a move vital to their continuing development. The two of them were totally disinterested in conventional instrumentation, and couldn't be bothered to take the time to learn how to play anyway.

It wasn't long before Ware and Craig-Marsh found a kindred spirit in the guise of a plastic surgery theatre porter called Phil Oakey, who again couldn't really play anything. But it wasn't long before the porter became a singer, the computer operators became synthesiser players and they called themselves The Human League.

They decided to present themselves as a multi-media combination and played along to backing tapes and a film and slide backdrop. They began to make

waves with a couple of independent singles, and it wasn't long before Virgin Records signed them up towards the end of the seventies.

They only met with moderate commercial success, and the cracks in the Human League began to show. In October 1980, Martyn Ware and Ian Craig-Marsh left to set up their own

production company called the British Electric Foundation (B.E.F.), while Phil Oakey and a couple of additional members soldiered on as the Human League.

It was during negotiations for the split that Ware and Craig-Marsh pulled off a master-stroke. They only agreed to relinquish the name the Human League in return for a share of future royalties, and when you consider how successful the Human League have been since, Ware and Craig-Marsh must be laughing all the way to the bank!

The twosome decided to make a clean break and moved down to London to work

"My Mum, Dad, brother and I all shared the same bedroom until I was eight. It's embarrassing to talk about it now, because people think you're exaggerating"

Glenn Gregory

on the B.E.F. project. Part of the plan was to conceive a trio to be called Heaven 17 after a fictitious group in Stanley Kubrick's film *A Clockwork Orange.*

Enter Glenn Gregory. He'd been working in London as a photographer and stage hand, and Ware and Craig-Marsh, remembering him from The Meatwhistle theatre group days, tracked him down and recruited him as vocalist for Heaven 17.

However from the outset, Ware was keen to distinguish between Heaven 17 and B.E.F.: *"B.E.F. will tend to be involved with more experimental projects, whereas Heaven 17 is a 100 per cent serious attempt to be incredibly popular."*

But Heaven 17 didn't get off to a very good start. In March 1981, they released their debut single **(We Don't Need This) Fascist Groove Thang,** and the BBC took great exception to the explicit political messages in the song, promptly banning it.

The group didn't seem to mind though as Martyn Ware pointed out: *"You can't be born in South Yorkshire, and not be a Socialist."*

Despite its lack of radio play, the watertight computer soul/funk mix proved irresistible for the dancefloor, and so with plenty of club support the single managed to tickle the lower end of the charts.

A couple more singles were released, again proving to be near misses. Then, early in 1982, Martyn and Ian decided to test their mettle as B.E.F. producers and put together a huge project called **Music Of Quality And Distinction.** Here they encouraged the likes of Tina Turner, Gary Glitter and Sandie Shaw (having been turned down by David Bowie and Scott Walker) to cover material made famous by other artists. Although it was a brave idea, it didn't meet with the expected critical and commercial response.

Martyn was disappointed with the criticism the LP attracted: *"I thought it was unfair. At least it was different, and we put a lot of money and effort into it. Reviews like that encourage you not to take risks."*

Still undeterred, B.E.F. struck gold when they teamed up Tina Turner with the Al Green classic **Let's Stay Together.** It was well received and became a big hit early in 1984. B.E.F. were truly in business.

The trio continued to make progress as Heaven 17 too. Their much acclaimed first album **Penthouse And Pavement** came out in the Autumn of 1982, and April of the next year saw the release of their second LP, **The Luxury Gap,** which has gone on to sell a half million copies worldwide. The LP also spawned their first major hit single **Temptation** featuring some fabulous vocals from former Isaac Hayes backing singer Carol Kenyon.

"Heaven 17 is a 100 per cent serious attempt to be incredibly popular"

Martyn Ware

The Luxury Gap also saw Heaven 17 play down their boardroom image to a level where they didn't seem to be too bothered about visual style. The songs though, continue to boom out the group's heartfelt opinions of life in the post-industrial age.

As Heaven 17's fascination with the new technology deepens, there seems to be little prospect of them playing live. Instead they prefer to project themselves through an intriguing set of videos, and anyway Martyn would much rather stay indoors as he explained: *"I fiddle for hours with my home computer, and monopolise the TV. Only problem is it drives my wife crazy, she can never watch any of her favourite programmes!"*

Yes, life can be so trying as you hurtle your way to the top of the pop pile!

HEAVEN 17

HUMAN LEAGUE

Intrigue, romance, struggle, a happy ending – the Human League story has it all. It's a chapter that will rank amongst pop's finest. A series of events that could only exist in the myth spinning world of modern music. Where else could a hospital porter way-lay two schoolgirls in a disco and incorporate them into a top synthesiser group?

Two 17-year-old girls, Joanne Catherall and Susanne Sulley, were regulars at Sheffield nightclub called **The Crazy Daisy Disco**, and – let's not beat about the bush – the League's main man, Phil Oakey, fancied Joanne. So what better way to win her heart than to ask her and her friend to join his pop group?

Joanne takes up the story: "*My Mother refused to let me join outright, but then Phil came round for Sunday lunch, and by the end of the afternoon convinced my parents that it wouldn't be such a bad idea after all.*"

Oakey, who only a few years previously was sweating it out as a hospital porter, had real problems on his hands. The Human League had just split into two factions, and his half were booked to go on a UK tour.

There had been numerous disagreements about the musical direction the group should follow and so founder-members Martyn Ware and Ian Craig-Marsh left to form Heaven 17 and a production company, the British Electric Foundation.

This meant that Oakey and fellow Leaguer Adrian Wright, the visual director, were left high and dry, and to cap it all, neither could play a musical instrument! To their credit they decided not to cancel the tour, but to augment their line-up – which is where we came in.

Besides recruiting the girls, the two men hired local bass player Ian Burden, who helped to hold the group together during the subsequent British live dates. Phil said later: "*I just knew we were going to be alright, because for some reason I felt that we were something special. I still don't really know why.*"

Part of the reason for the Human League's continued success must be the fact that they had a solid past to build on. Tracks like **Being Boiled** and the **Holiday 80** collection had attracted much attention, the latter even flirting with the charts in 1980.

It didn't take long for Joanne and Susanne to prove their worth, because it was they who convinced Oakey to release **The Sound Of The Crowd,** which was the group's first substantial hit, reaching Number 12 in the Summer of 1981. And this paved the way for Oakey's semi-autobiographical **Love Action,** which went into the top three, a couple of months later.

It was at this point that Jo Callis who had previously contributed on the writing front, joined the group full-time. He had already found some success as guitarist with Scottish band **The Rezillos,** and he provided the much needed impetus for new material.

However the new members that supplemented the Oakey/Wright axis in the group were not to have equal shares. As Callis commented later: *"Phil and Adrian own the name The Human League. They employ the rest of us on a contract basis."*

"I used to be a highly immoral person. I was going out with another girl, and telling lies to my wife."

Phil Oakey

There was now no stopping the six-piece Human League, as they hit the top ten again with **Open Your Heart** in the Autumn of 1981. The best was yet to come. Their eagerly awaited debut LP **Dare** became the top selling LP on both sides of the Atlantic. A feat repeated by their next single **Don't You Want Me,** which boasted one of the best opening lines in recent pop history – *"You were working as a waitress in a cocktail bar . . ."*

Dare went on to sell over two and a half million copies worldwide, and very important, tore open the conservative US market. Along with acts like Culture Club, Duran Duran and Spandau Ballet, the Human League became part of the much publicised British invasion, but it wasn't all plain sailing for Oakey and co.

After **Don't You Want Me** went multi-platinum, the group had high expectations for **Love Action,** the follow-up, but it barely managed to scrape the bottom of the US chart. And the reason? The androgynous picture of Phil Oakey on the cover of **Dare,** which was released between the two singles, outraged Middle America, and sales slumped. Attitudes have softened since then, though, and once again the group find themselves well placed.

Back at home the Human League rounded off a great year with a Motown flavoured synth single called **Mirror Man,** which peaked at Number Two in the charts. Then . . . nothing!

There followed an 18 month stint away from the limelight, while the group parted company with regular producer Martin Rushent, who many believe masterminded their distinctive synthesiser sound.

It was a time when the boys and girls could devote more time to their private lives. Oakey brought his romance with Joanne Catherall out into the open, and admitted to the press: *"I used to be a highly immoral person. I was going out with another girl, and telling lies to my wife."* He has since split from his spouse and set up home with Joanne.

There was also another well publicised romance within the band. Backing singer Susanne Sulley courted Mike Nolan from Bucks Fizz for a lengthy period until they parted in mid-1983, Mike blaming pressure of work for the split. The extended break also gave Oakey time to indulge in his passion for motorbikes, an interest totally at odds with the fey image he presents as a pop star. The centre piece of his collection is the much prized

silver BMW, and he often terrorises the citizens of Sheffield tearing up and down the road on it!

The Spring of 1984 saw the six-piece re-emerge with veteran producer Chris Thomas, whose past credits include work for The Pretenders and Roxy Music. This combination (along with additional producer Hugh Padgham, called in to finish and re-mix after Thomas ran out of time), delivered the long awaited follow-up to **Dare,** a varied and lively bunch of songs under the collective title of **Hysteria.**

Their first single from this, **The Lebanon,** heralded a new direction in composition. Here, they pinpointed life in that war torn area of the Middle East – subject matter much loftier than the boy meets girl songs on **Dare.** It was also their least successful single since **The Sound Of The Crowd.**

Phil Oakey also sprang back from seclusion with a new hairstyle. Gone was the lop-sided long and short affair he'd sported earlier, in favour of a more symmetrical long cut. He even went unshaven on TV appearances, which added to the more manly new look.

So, in the relatively short time that they've been together, the Human League have emerged as *the* top synthesiser band around. Fairly ironic then, that their record company, Virgin, told Phil Oakey in the early days that synthesiser groups stood little or no chance of success. By the time the **Dare** LP hit the Number One slot in Britain and the US, Virgin had no recollection of ever making that statement!

● Jo Callis, Phil Oakey, Susanne Sulley, Adrian Wright, Joanne Catherall and Ian Burden

MICHAEL JACKSON

● From the Thriller video

Michael Jackson is the biggest star in the world.

As lead singer with the Jackson 5, he and his brothers made up one of the most popular acts of the seventies. Now as a solo artist, Michael is the biggest thing since the Beatles and the greatest single phenomenon since Elvis Presley.

In 16 months Michael Jackson's **Thriller** LP became the biggest selling album of all time with over 33 million copies sold. It swept the board at the American Music Awards and won an unprecedented eight Grammy Awards – the music industry's Oscars.

Since its release in December 1982, it has broken all records. The next edition of *The Guinness Book Of Records* will show that seven of the album's nine tracks have made the American top 10 as singles. The six singles in Britain have all made the top 20 and have contributed to a further 20 million records sold worldwide.

The album has been a runaway success. If you added the worldwide sales of 1983's heavyweight albums: David Bowie's **Let's Dance**, Police's **Synchronicity**, Culture Club's **Colour By Numbers**, Duran Duran's **Seven And The Ragged Tiger**, Paul McCartney's **Pipes Of Peace**, Spandau Ballet's **True**, Elton John's **Too Low For Zero** and The Rolling Stones' **Undercover**, you would only just be equalling the astonishing popularity of Jackson's **Thriller.**

The record is unstoppable.

Scarcely a week has gone by since the release of the record that a trade or consumer music paper didn't carry a Michael Jackson story detailing another sales milestone – whether it be Best Selling Compact Disc Of All Time, Best Selling Video Of All Time and so on.

Barely a day goes by without a national daily logging some bizarre quirk that the super-rich star has indulged in. 'Wacko Jacko' headlines abound, depicting the singer as living in the twilight zone of reality, totally wrapped up in daydream fantasies.

It seems almost every hour someone in the media is talking about Michael Jackson – either to praise him or to use him as the yardstick that everybody must match up to. He has become the perfect enigma. He's the person everybody knows a lot about, but nobody knows at all.

There must be bookmakers all over the world breathing a sigh of relief. Can you guess the odds they would have offered on an energetic 11-year-old, with big, soulful eyes and a voice that could bulldoze mountains, becoming the biggest star in the world 15 years later?

Everybody knew that Michael was a special talent when the glissando strings of **I Want You Back** heralded the first sparkling hit of the Jackson 5 in 1969. But nobody could have foretold that 15 years on he'd have proved his longevity as a top pop attraction, *and* be the Number One influence on the whole field of pop music, despite being barely older than his current chart contemporaries

But don't believe that Michael has devastated his rivals on talent alone. Sure, he has that quality in abundance, but it's been allied to a fierce dedication, and intuitive understanding of the mechanics of mythmaking and the ability to galvinise his energy into one spellbinding flash of brilliance. With so much to offer it hasn't been difficult for, first, Tamla Motown and, later, the might of the giant CBS corporation, to create a legend just when you thought the star system was dead.

Michael was born on August 29, 1958, the seventh child of Joe and Katherine Jackson's nine-strong brood from Gary, Indiana.

Joe had always had a dream – he wanted to play music. But the children made him defer the dream – until he caught third child Tito (born October 15, 1953) playing with his guitar. When he found Tito could actually play, the dream was rekindled. He rehearsed his eldest boys, Jackie (born May 4, 1951), Tito, Jermaine (born December 11, 1954); and later added Marlon (born March 12, 1957) and little Michael.

MICHAEL JACKSON

Michael was only five-years-old, but he rapidly developed into a tiny, apple-cheeked dynamo. He could, like today, explode in a dazzling, pyrotechnic display of dancing and singing.

Rehearsals took up all Michael's toddlerhood, gigging til five in the morning, then being expected to keep up his grades occupied his early childhood, and being a star has taken up the rest of his life.

After a hard, five year slog of winning talent contests and supporting artists like the Chi-Lites, Temptations, Gladys Knight and the Pips and Jackie Wilson, Michael had learnt his craft. By the time the group landed their contract with Berry Gordy's Motown Records, Michael was a veteran aged 11. He'd been singing for over half his life.

The Jackson 5 was the last gasp for the conveyer belt system of record making, that had made Motown synonymous with good music all over the world. The company was about to be dragged into the seventies, with Stevie Wonder and Marvin Gaye leading the way to more direct control over their careers. But the system that had made names like Diana Ross, The Supremes, Four Tops, Temptations, Martha Reeves and the Vandellas, Gladys Knight and countless others was used to full effect on Michael and his brothers.

They were put through the famous Motown grooming school for a year. They worked on Michael's choreography to smooth out the more overt James Brown mannerisms and help him gel better with his brothers.

They were taught not to be controversial in interviews – the art of saying a lot and saying nothing at all.

The natural enthusiasm of the kids was slowly suppressed. First Joe and then Motown had put the dampers on their cheeky charm, pressuring them to be perfect. It inevitably made Michael secretive. His sense of fun and mischief in the early days make a staggering contrast to the painfully shy adult that is adored the world over.

I Want You Back, their debut single was released in America in autumn 1969, after a year of being refined by Motown. It was one of the most powerful debuts ever. The record was an aural steamroller. It took off like a rocket and exploded with a nervous, frenetic energy. It was hooked on the voice – a child's soprano – but steeped in the experience and phrasing of a mature adult. It hit the heart, feet and soul with devastating accuracy.

The Jackson 5's first four singles in America – **I Want You Back, ABC, The Love You Save,** and **I'll Be There** – all reached Number One in 1970 and sold an astonishing two million copies each. The boys occupied the Number One slot for two and a half months out of nine.

Over the next three years the Jackson 5 became the biggest selling act in Motown's considerable history. Single-handedly they became responsible for the teeny-bopper phenomenon, sprouting a host of imitators from the Osmonds to David Cassidy's Partridge Family.

But by 1974 the Motown machine was seizing up. The hit formulas of the sixties had no place in the mid-seventies and the Jackson 5 were being pushed into the Las Vegas circuit. With the addition of brother Randy (born October 29, 1962) and sisters LaToya and Janet, they became a 'family group' in the worst sense of the term, complete with comedy sketches.

But wily Joe Jackson realised that Motown had straitjacketed his sons. He realised that Michael's solo career, which had produced four top 10 hits in 1972 in Britain – **Got To Be There, Rockin' Robin, Ain't No Sunshine** and **Ben** – was being stifled. So he took the boys to Epic Records in 1976. Jermaine decided to remain at Motown for a fitful solo career, but was replaced by Randy in the full line-up. The boys were also made to leave behind their Jackson 5 name and became The Jacksons.

They immediately had success with

producers Gamble and Huff – responsible for the Philly boom of the previous years. **Enjoy Yourself** was a million selling hit worldwide in 1976. **Show You The Way To Go** was the Jacksons' first UK Number One in 1977. Their debut CBS album called **The Jacksons** was the first that allowed them to write their own songs.

It was only after their third album, **Destiny,** in 1979 (which produced the million selling **Shake Your Body (Down To The Ground)**), and after Michael had starred in the musical film *The Wiz,* that Michael began to pick up the pieces of his solo career.

Using the production talents of veteran producer Quincy Jones and the songwriting and arranging intuition of British born Rod Temperton from Heatwave, Michael released **Off The Wall** in 1979.

"I want to prove I can make it on my own," he said, *"that my talent doesn't depend on anyone else."*

All four singles – **Don't Stop 'Til You Get Enough, Rock With You** (both US Number Ones), **Off The Wall** and **She's Out Of My Life** – reached the top 10 in both Britain and America between 1979 and 1980. A fifth single **Girlfriend** – also charted in Britain. The album made musical history for that achievement.

The album sold eight million worldwide, each single sold over a million and Michael won a Grammy for his performance on **Don't Stop 'Til You Get Enough.**

Jackson-mania had returned and Michael was suddenly the hottest property in the world again. In 1980 a TV show proclaimed that The Jacksons (solo, as a group and as the Jackson 5) were the largest selling group after The Beatles, claiming a staggering 93 million records sold worldwide.

Anything by Michael Jackson sold. Motown released a vintage song called **One Day In Your Life** in Britain and the ballad gave Michael his first solo Number One in 1981. The Jacksons' vastly underrated fourth album **Triumph** spawned another four hits between 1980-1.

It's obvious that Michael uses his fantasy world as a means of keeping pressure away from himself. He goes insane to stay sane. He can afford to indulge in every whim he's never had the time before to exploit. Those around him are aware that he is a special talent and are only too keen to help him stay that way.

He's also shrewd enough to realise that people want the mystery kept in their stars. He long ago learned the appeal of keeping something back from the public.

His image of the single glittering glove is taken directly from Walt Disney characters and it's this mass appeal Michael has sought and gained.

He's realised that film is a medium he can control to the finest pitch and that a performance can be captured, at its peak, forever. So it is that Michael has been the most successful artist of the pop video age.

All of his promos have been memorable song and dance spectaculars that have been the standard everybody else must aspire to, with videos like **Billy Jean, Beat It** and the £700,000 14-minute horror movie spoof **Thriller**.

Through the easily controlled media of records and film, Michael has stamped his undeniable style and unbounded talents across the whole spectrum of entertainment.

The only frightening aspect of his success is the impression that at 26-years-old he is just starting to flex his muscles. There's no doubt Michael Jackson is going to be the one to watch, well into the next century.

His whole life is insulated from reality. His friends — many of them celebrities like Jane Fonda, Liza Minnelli, Brooke Shields, Diana Ross and Paul McCartney — help keep his illusions close at hand.

So how does this bizarre lifestyle square with his tough reputation as a hard-headed business negotiator; a man who oversees every aspect of his career from his top royalty rate for albums — the biggest in the industry at some 46 per cent of the wholesale price — to the smallest sequins on his stage costumes?

Easy, it's business. It's a world Michael has been brought up in and he's comfortable in. He knows what he wants and can easily get it. He's been a millionaire since he was 14 and his current personal fortune is well over $100 million.

But it was the release of **Thriller** that turned a steady stream of world interest into a swollen torrent of obsession about Michael's lifestyle.

The boy who never had a childhood had tried to create a private corner for his unbearably public life. The result is a solitary existence behind the closed doors of his mock-Tudor mansion in Encino, California.

Here Michael has created his own amusement park. He has a mini zoo, a hugh stock of movies, a video games arcade, a Disneyland-created room of animated models, a vast collection of cartoon films, an electric car from another Disneyland ride, an ice-cream cart and a room full of shop window mannequins — the friends he wasn't allowed to cultivate as a child, with whom he has fantasy conversations.

Couple his withdrawn public behaviour with the fact that he barely eats, rarely leaves home, except to attend his Jehovah's Witness Kingdom Hall or to visit his favourite vegetarian restaurant, and you've got the sort of enigma the gossip columnists find irresistible.

MICHAEL JACKSON

HOWARD JONES

possible touring because of his love for the stage and his awareness that his music and mime are best shown off in a live act. He believes that the success of his songs is mainly due to the lyrics. His ability to write in song the thoughts and pains of the average man in the street comes from his strong desire to communicate with people.

His reputation for being a natural nice guy was recently enhanced by some of his ex-workmates, who clubbed together and had a plaque made and fitted to the machine he used to operate on the production line of a cling-film factory, only months before his first hit.

This is just the beginning of the Howard Jones story. The man has so much more to say with his music, his career can only continue to go from strength to strength.

HOWARD JONES

1983 was a year that Howard Jones will never forget. His first two singles made the top ten, he was voted Best New Artist in two major music papers, he had sell out concerts and hits in America, Sweden, Germany and Belgium.

Howard was born in Southampton in 1955, but was constantly being moved, not only from house to house, but also country to country, because his father was continually changing his job. He took piano lessons soon after he'd learned to walk, and joined his first band at the age of 15. Four years later, he went to music college in Manchester, but soon gave that up as a bad job.

His musical outlook changed dramatically when he discovered how to use synthesisers, previously having done most of his playing on an electric piano. He started appearing as a solo artist in a few local venues in his home town, High Wycombe, then decided he wanted to involve his audience more with what has been described as a music hall-come-pantomime approach to illustrate his songs. For this he invited dance expressionist, Jed Hoile, to perform some of Howard's songs in mime and costume. Hoile is now an integral part of the act, not only on stage, but also on TV.

Howard believes that communication is of the highest importance. When on stage, he feels that there should be no barrier between the artist and the audience.

From the pubs and clubs in the Buckinghamshire area, Howard's first big break came via a session for John Peel on Radio One. This was so well received, it was repeated many times on various other programmes on the network. From that, came support slots on tours of OMD and China Crisis.

Still without ever having any sort of record release even on a small independent, he was signed by WEA in the Summer of 1983, and his first single,

● Dance expressionist Jed Hoile (right) is an integral part of Howard's live act.

New Song, climbed to the Number Three spot in the British charts and established him as one of the country's most important newcomers, with top TV appearances, press interviews and packed houses for his live shows.

His second single What Is Love? was an even bigger success, reaching the Number Two position and firmly establishing the Howard Jones synth-based music amongst British record buyers.

After two hit singles in 1983, he bounded back into the charts at the start of 1984 with his third single Hide And Seek. This was followed closely by the release of his first album Human's Lib, which had the rare distinction of entering the LP charts immediately at Number One.

Howard spends as much time as

NiK KeRSHAW

Nicholas David Kershaw's parents had no idea when he was born that they would have a) such a famous son, and b) such a diminutive one. After all, he looked pretty much like all the rest of the babies around Bristol at the time, most of whom are now bank clerks, pickets, dentists or standing in a dole queue – and most of them over five foot four inches.

Mind you, he's seven stone heavier than he was on March 1st back in 1958. His baby blue eyes haven't changed much, although his brown hair has acquired a few blonde highlights in recent months. Shortly after Nik was born, the family moved to Ipswich. He went to the local primary school and later attended Northgate Grammar School, where he excelled in art and rugby (or should that read rug making).

With some school friends he formed a group and named it Half Pint Hog – no doubt a good humoured dig at himself. They played three gigs and disbanded. Having failed as a musician, there was no alternative but to take a legitimate job, and this he did for three years in the Ipswich Department Of Employment. However it was difficult not to listen to music as both his parents were musicians – though of a different genre: Evelyn, his mother, ran a local choir, Douglas, his father was a flautist.

By now, his older brother, Jonathan had become a dolphin trainer and an eccentric, both of which made Nik feel boringly normal. So he handed in his notice to the Department Of Employment and then went outside to join the dole queue! In fact he formed another band. The music was jazz/rock orientated and so they called themselves Fusion. They became well known in the Ipswich area, but could not break out of the parochial mould.

Whilst many of Nik's friends were listening to Gilbert O'Sullivan or the Carpenters, he was into much stronger stuff like Ritchie Blackmore and Alice Cooper, and it took some persuading to get a few mates to go with him to see The

Pink Fairies when they appeared at the Manor Ballroom in Ipswich.

You could say, seeing this, his first live show, was the turning point in his life. (Although he did play Tweedledum with the Co-Op drama group at the YMCA a few weeks earlier). He was also into sta-press trousers and Elton John. The first record he ever bought was **Your Song** and today those early influences can be heard in his music. Particularly sta-press trousers.

Eventually Fusion de-fused and Nik decided to take a year off to concentrate on writing and leisure pursuits. He wrote a lot, saw his favourite films, *Marathon Man* and *Close Encounters Of The Third Kind,* and made himself sick on his favourite food, rhubarb flavoured yoghurt. He also spent a lot of time watching television and playing computer chess with his live-in girlfriend Sheri — something he still enjoys doing, but not with his girlfriend, with his wife: he married Sheri in 1983.

His social life was great, but he was becoming frustrated and depressed over his writing which he felt wasn't getting anywhere. He knew his songs were good and he was developing into an all round musician having become proficient in guitar, keyboards and percussive instruments. So as a last resort, although in his heart he thought it a waste of time, he put an advert in *Melody Maker* for a manager. He received nine replies from 'loonies' and one from Nine

> "I've learnt to make the demos as good as I can because a lot of people in the music business haven't got an awful lot of imagination".
>
> *Nik Kershaw*

Below Zero's ex-manager, Mickie Modern.

It was love at first sight, and in a matter of days Mickie had signed him to MCA records, who rush released the first single **Don't Let The Sun Go Down,** which nibbled at the lower end of the charts AND hit much bigger on it's re-release in the summer of '84.

It was enough to start a buzz around the business that a major new talent was about to emerge. Mickie bought Nik a Porta-studio, which he keeps in his back bedroom. It does the job. Peter Collins, his producer, knows what he's getting at anyway. All his ideas are worked out on this initially before actually laying down tracks in the grown-up studio.

The second single **Wouldn't It Be Good** went to Number Four in the charts and Nik found himself a somewhat bemused overnight sensation. Rugby players are meant to be attractive to women, but never had he experienced anything like the adulation he was now getting. He found it exceedingly unnerving and wondered if he shouldn't perhaps join his brother and learn to communicate with dolphins instead. He's now realising, however, that communicating with people IS gratifying and indeed his ambition is to get his music across to as many people as possible.

Despite his touring Europe, (which he hopes will emulate the huge success of his first British tour), working on the new album and supporting Elton John at Wembley, he still finds time to pursue his hobby, photography, watch his favourite T.V. programmes like *Fawlty Towers, The Young Ones* and *The Comic Strip,* and go for country drives in his BMW with Sheri.

They still live in the Ipswich area and enjoy going with friends to local restaurants (particularly Indian), rather than London's latest in-clubs. He enjoys good conversation with intelligent, quiet, sensible people and steers clear of bigots and people who try to tell him how to run his life, when they haven't got their own sorted out.

One thing is for certain, Nik Kershaw will never have to go to the Ministry of Employment again.

NiK KERSHAW

CYNDI LAUPER

Cyndi Lauper does not lie about her age. She simply refuses to answer such impertinent questions with a dismissive shrug, a cavernous glimpse of her teeth masquerading under the guise of her infamous Hollywood smile and, if pressed further, a snarled riposte: *"What am I, a car?"*

It has taken Cyndi 31 years to become an overnight success; two decades full of being laughed at; being told she could not sing; that she was the ultimate loser. In 1984 her **She's So Unusual** album has taken up permanent residence in the American top ten. Singles like **Girls Just Want To Have Fun** and **Time After Time** (a US Number One) have been international hits.

This time last year American chat show host Johnny Carson had never heard of a Cyndi Lauper. Now her natural gift for comedy and an incredible voice ranging through four octaves keep him

glued to his leather armchair. Back home Cyndi is the biggest and brightest female singing star to emerge in an age. In Britain she is still considered to be a novelty act – a Tracey Ullman with a funny haircut and an incomprehensible accent.

Although she was born in Brooklyn on June 20, 1953, Cyndi grew up in Ozone Park, Queens – another of New York City's boroughs.

Queens bears as much resemblance to Manhattan as Croydon does to the West End of London. Queens does not swing, it staggers along, imparting to its native sons the ability to massacre the English language every time they open their mouths.

"My speaking voice," Cyndi admits in tones that would have Donald Duck

reaching for a throat spray in horror, *"is ridiculous."*

Her father, a shipping clerk whose interests ranged from archaeology to playing the xylophone, divorced her Catholic mother when Cyndi was five, leaving her to bring up three children by working 14 hour days in diners. Now her mother stars in Cyndi's videos and is stopped in the local streets.

She was expelled from a convent after six horrendous months and dropped out of art school. At this time she was heavily into vintage forties and fifties clothing; returning home from school, other children would bombard her with rocks. Aged 17, she packed and left Ozone Park for ever. Or so she thought.

Accompanied by her dog Sparkle – also a video star – she headed for the

woods north of Toronto, another Dorothy in a modern update of *The Wizard of Oz.* Homesick and probably suffering from malnutrition, she headed back for the Big Apple, working along the way as a painting class model and a pedlar of karate lessons – about which she knew nothing.

Today Cyndi reckons that all that bumming around was just an attempt to avoid her fate. She was always going to be a singer. From the very beginning. At five, she would sing two parts in *South Pacific,* changing her voice for each one. It was hardly surprising that her first real singing job was in bands playing Janis Joplin, Rod Stewart and Rolling Stones covers in bars around Long Island.

Her imitative power and range are still apparent today, when she drops instantly from a precious high fluting squeak to a rumbling husky growl that can raise the hackles at fifty paces.

But by 1977 her voice had been reduced to a croak and specialists were telling her she would never sing again. Some ignorant bar owners out on the Island never thought she could in the first place. With the aid of a voice coach Cyndi got her singing back and added something else – charisma.

The next step was fronting Blue Angel, a sort of rockabilly punk outfit. They released a superb album in 1980, that in Cyndi's parlance *"shipped lead and sold less."* It stiffed. Blue Angel collapsed in a welter of recrimination between record company (Polygram) and the band's manager.

Cyndi's major live performance in 1983 took place in court. Along with other members of the band, in an attempt to free themselves of restrictive contracts, she filed for bankruptcy. It was granted and she was free to start again, aged 30.

"The judge said 'Let the canary sing'," says Cyndi, "And sing she did."

And sing she has. But it is not just her voice and the inspired covers of Prince's **When You Were Mine,** the Brains' epic **Money Changes Everything** – something of a Lauper philosophy – or the weeping **Time After Time** that has made **She's So Unusual** a multi-million seller. Somehow Cyndi Lauper has made a square foot of vinyl and cardboard reek of personality. That is why she is a big star.

Cyndi may look a little bizarre. Her clothes seem to be haphazardly strung together with the fashion awareness of a colour blind ironmonger lost in the Borneo jungle since the Second World War. She has the dainty poise of a runaway Sherman tank. On stage she wanders around the boards in an aimless zigzag that somehow avoids demolishing the drum kit.

She is not dressing that way to sell records, but because she feels comfortable. She is naturally funny. Her humour is self-deprecating without falling into parody.

Cyndi attributes her success to the PIG principle as taught to her by her mentor Captain Lu, an ex-wrestler she met on a flight from Puerto Rico.

"The PIG Principle is nothing deep. It is just Politeness, Integrity with a little bit of intelligence and Grooming. That's what Captain Lu tells me and he is an authority on grooming."

Captain Lu is not just a figment of Cyndi's imagination. He can be seen in her videos, along with her mother, her brother Butch and her dog Sparkle and a cast of thousands` of bizarre friends picked up when she was singing in a Japanese restaurant, or working in a vintage clothes' store. All parts of a past that has become a very lucrative present.

Cyndi Lauper's PIG Principle will never be taught at a Swiss finishing school. The head mistress would never let her through the gates. Not that she could care.

America has been waiting for someone like Cyndi for an age, a rock singer with a sense of humour to match Dolly Parton. It may take longer to convince the blasé Europeans that there is more to her than a girl who just wants to have fun and does it by looking silly.

Cyndi Lauper is a natural. Now watch her fly.

CYNDI LAUPER
C

LIMAHL

Never having been to Wigan I always associated it with cloth caps and hob nailed boots, after the comic strip character of yesteryear, Ernie Entwistle. But having met Limahl, the scales have dropped from my eyes and I am now prepared to believe that everyone in Wigan walks about in designer jeans with spiked two tone hair, styled in the northern branch of Michaeljohn.

Limahl may no longer live in Wigan, but his parents, Cynthia and Eric Hamill, older brothers Paul and Anthony, not to mention dozens of cousins, do. They still think of him as 'our Christopher', although younger sister Caroline, who shares his Swiss Cottage flat, has stopped looking over her shoulder when someone shouts "Limahl".

He was born on December 19th in 1958 – just in time to hear Conway Twitty singing his Number One hit **It's Only Make Believe.** He would argue he doesn't remember, but it could be that's what inspired him to become an actor many years later. Meanwhile, back in the real world, Christopher Hamill attended Wigan's Nesnes High School, and because he had a crush on the teacher, excelled at English. And because he was – and still is – only five foot six inches, and weighing eight and a half stone, he *didn't* excel at long-jumping.

Conway Twitty's inspiring message was still subliminal to the 17-year-old Wigan lad, who took a series of boring jobs in boutiques and clubs. It got through round in 1977, when he joined the Westcliffe-On-Sea, Palace Theatre Repertory Company. Lots of parts followed including *Aladin*, Lamar in *Godspell* and months of touring with *Joseph's Technicolour Dreamcoat*.

The thespian bit lasted for three years, then he formed a short-lived punk group called **Vox Deus.** Next Limahl joined **Crossword** but left to form **Brooks** with Mike Nolan (later of Bucks Fizz). They were managed by Frea Miller, who never did for them what she has since done for Shakin' Stevens. Again things didn't work out and it was back to the Embassy club for a spot of 'waiting'.

He didn't have to wait for long before he met up with Nick Beggs and a songwriting partnership was formed, eventually resulting in Kajagoogoo. Even though their first single **Too Shy** established them overnight, the press gave them a hard time. EMI were accused of 'manufacturing' them and the boys were written off as puppets. Few journalists mentioned the fact that Limahl had a long and varied musical background, preferring to speculate, instead, on his relationship with Radio One's Paul Gambaccini.

Despite the animosity, Kajagoogoo were flavour of the week, appearing on almost every music magazine front cover and television programme, proving that fans do not give a toss about Fleet Street. However all good things must come to an end and Kajagoogoo said goodbye to Limahl. The reasons given are the usual 'conflicting musical opinions, but we are still good friends' type of thing. Rod Stewart's astute ex-manager, Billy Gaff, saw Limahl's potential as a unique solo artiste and signed him to his management company, Riva.

Stripped now of a supportive group, Limahl spent weeks crafting his beautifully constructed songs. His lyrics are exquisite in their political and social awareness. He draws on the outpourings of other artists, from playwright to painter, at the same time honing his own emotional and intellectual thoughts.

But it's not all Jean Jacques Rousseau and Shakespeare, Limahl has been known to go to the Hippodrome and the odd club occasionally. However don't expect ever to catch him off his guard, because he only drinks orange juice — which goes well with the vegetarian food he eats. And when he's not absorbing all that culture he enjoys films like *Alien* and anything with Roger Moore or Dyan

> "*Everyone is looking for something in life. I think you find it and lose it. And I think most people have – they've found it and lost it.*"

Cannon. As is to be expected he hates war and hate. Or to re-phrase that – he is a pacifist and romantic, not to mention a dog and cat lover (but he's not keen on squirrels).

1984 saw a world promotional tour, which included Australia, Japan and Los Angeles. However Limahl says his favourite place is Zermatt in Switzerland. When in Japan, he entered for the Japanese Tokyo Music Festival and came third with **Only For Love**. He won a trophy and £1000. He recorded the title song, written by Giorgio Moroder, for a sci-fi film entitled, *The Never Ending Story*. He is currently writing and preparing for a possible round the world concert tour.

Limahl's involvement with Kajagoogoo has proved something of a handicap, because being part of such a blatantly commercial group, no one thought to listen to him on a serious level. They, of course, might say the same of him.

Discography:

| Singles: | Only For Love | LML 1 |
| | Too Much Trouble | LML 2 |

| Album: | Don't Suppose EJ 2401561 |

All tracks written by Limahl
All tracks produced by Tim Palmer and De Harris

With Kajagoogoo
Album: White Feathers
Worldwide hit: Too Shy

L·I·M·a·H·L

MADNESS

1984 has been a crucial year in the life of Britain's top singles band – Madness. After 19 consecutive top 20 singles and five years, they've lost key member Mike Barson – the foundation stone on whom their success was built – and their deal with Stiff Records – whose drive and imagination made them one of Britain's most popular combos – has come to an end.

1984 is the year the 'Nutty Boys' finally got serious.

It seems like a long time since the dancing Two-Tone man – shades, skinny tie, pork-pie hat and pumping elbows – heralded a brand new group. It was August 10, 1979 that saw the first release, **The Prince,** zip up the charts to Number 16 and unleash the seven diverse personalities that made up the group on the welcoming public.

The band was formed late 1976 at the home of Mike 'Barso' Barson (born April 21, 1958). Two other mates from Gospel Oak School in Camden, North London, joined him to form the Invaders. They were Lee 'Kix' Thompson (born October 5, 1957) and Chris 'Chrissie Boy' Foreman (born August 8, 1955).

"We were just mates living near each other in Kentish Town," recalls Chris. *"Mike had a piano ... Lee had a sax ... and I bought a guitar."*

It took another three years and many personnel changes before they officially became Madness in 1979. The changes are well documented on the inner sleeve of their second album **Absolutely.**

Leader Barson had recruited Graham 'Suggs' McPherson (born January 13, 1961) on vocals; Mark 'Bedders' Bedford (born August 24, 1961) on bass; Daniel 'Woody' Woodgate (born October 19, 1960) on drums; and a curious lad who used to dance on stage with them, providing the visuals before he became a vocalist. His name was Carl 'Chas Smash' Smythe (born January 14, 1958).

Madness built up a reputation on the London pub circuit, until one day in March 1979 Suggs saw Coventry band The Specials at a Rock Against Racism gig at the Hope and Anchor. He was amazed to see them ploughing the same rock'n'reggae hybrid. An alliance developed, leading to shared gigs and an opportunity for Madness to release a single on the new label The Specials were setting up. The single was **The Prince** – a tribute to Jamaican Blue Beat king Prince Buster.

The whole Two-Tone package – racially integrated dance style with its roots in reggae and ska – identified the common concerns of the depressed youth cultures. The Specials, Madness and Selecter were the tonic for the post-punk troops. While the other two bands became more politicised, Madness presented anarchic humour with the West Indian beat and called it The Nutty Sound.

The music business became aroused by the Two-Tone buzz in the summer of '79.

"There were lots of companies after us," said one band member later. *"Magnet, Island, Virgin, Sire, EMI — they'd all heard we were supposed to be 'the next big thing', but couldn't quite see how or why. They bought us lunches, but we weren't impressed."*

They eventually signed to Stiff – the independent label that was showing the majors how to get hits at the time.

MADNESS

"Stiff stood out a mile because of their attitude. They didn't try to hand us any bullshit. Dave Robinson (managing director) took us to the pub next door and spoke to us realistically. He understood what we were doing and had plans for us. All the other companies just wanted a ska band because they were currently hip. He saw how we could develop. He was just like a father to us!"

It was a marriage made in heaven. The self-styled 'world's most flexible label' relished marketing the young band with the memorable and eye-catching campaigns that had been their trademark from the days of Elvis Costello, Ian Dury and The Damned. The band's originality and humour, which suited the mood of the period, made it an irresistible commodity to pop fans.

But more than that, there was something of substance behind the wacky posturing. While the crazy roller-coaster line up on the sleeve of their debut album **One Step Beyond** set the scene for the madcap antics of the north Londoners, it was their third single, **My Girl,** that showed they had a craftsman's touch with the single format.

"There was never any question of having a couple of hits and then being washed up and forgotten."

Madness swooped to stardom with total assurance, modifying their output and image to outlive most of their contempories.

"There was never any question of having a couple of hits and then being washed up and forgotten."

There was no chance of that. Their

● Kix, Chas Smash, Suggs, Bedders (Barso behind him), Chrissie Boy and Woody

debut album spent nearly a year in the British top 75 after its release in October 1979. The single of the same title – their second – spent three months on the chart, peaking at Number Seven.

My Girl reached Number Three at the turn of the decade and set the standard over the next four years.

Madness's next seven single releases made the top 10 over the following two years: **Work Rest And Play** EP (April 6, 1980), **Baggy Trousers** (September 3, 1980), **Embarrassment** (November 4, 1980), **The Return Of The Las Palmas Seven** (January 7, 1981), **Grey Day** (April 4, 1981), **Shut Up** (September 7, 1981) and **It Must Be Love,** which hit Number Four in December 1981.

They didn't do too badly at having hit albums either – so often the stumbling block for singles bands. The second album **Absolutely,** reached Number Two soon after release in September 1980, spending 41 weeks in the charts.

October 1981 saw the release of their third album **Seven.** This reached Number Five. But already they were thinking of expanding. The same month saw the release of a full-length feature film called **Take It Or Leave It.**

It was a natural move. So much of the vibrancy of Madness had reached the public through an ingenious series of lunatic videos. Each vignette compounded the image of cockney Marx Brothers played at 78rpm. No other British band used the fledgling video movement with such a consistent vision and invention.

Unfortunately the film, though interesting, couldn't sustain the Madness universe and opted for a documentary style piece about the founding of the band.

But their later **Complete Madness** video collection, released simultaneously

with a greatest hits record collection of the same name in April 1982, did the band justice. The album, video and single **House Of Fun** all reached the pinnacles of their respective charts and mark the peak of Madness.

The hit machine continued with the more sombre album **The Rise And Fall** in November and single, **Our House,** which reached Number Five. The song later won an Ivor Novello award for Best Pop Song. It was to prove even more important as the record that gave Madness a top 10 hit in America in July 1983.

With every single during 1983 going to the British top 10, it seemed they could do no wrong. But on December 21, Mike Barson announced that he was leaving the band to set up home in Amsterdam with his Dutch wife Sandra. In a farewell message the other band members said: "The mild mannered foundation stone will be sorely missed by Madness with sadness."

The band released **Michael Caine** in January 1984 – a single featuring the voice of the cockney actor. The band's sixth album, **Keep Moving** was noted for its serious mood and won lavish critical acclaim. It entered the British albums top 10 in its first week.

With the single **One Better Day,** released in May 1984, the band announced that they would be seeking fresher recording pastures as their agreement with Stiff had expired.

With the charting of **One Better Day,** Madness are second only to Cliff Richard in maintaining a 100 per cent top 20 strike with this their 19th single. But whether they can top his 31 consecutive top 20 hits depends on how much of a gap is left by Mike Barson's departure and how much a new record company will stimulate them to higher achievements.

NEW ORDER

However grisly it may sound, New Order's birth – and subsequent success – rests on the swinging shoulders of a suicide. New Order's previous incarnation had been as Joy Division, a band of legendary status who were responsible for an atmospheric style of playing often defined as 'doom rock'.

Fronted by the wan figure of Ian Curtis, they released two LP's, **Unknown Pleasures** and **Closer,** on the seminal Northern label, Factory. Their music was heavily scored by Curtis' harrowing and doleful nature – a sensibility that captured the souls of any who felt an affinity with this stark and stormy mental landscape. It was almost inevitable then that the final seal on Joy Division's monopoly of sadness would be the death of Curtis. Prone to epileptic fits (he had already attempted suicide twice) and reeling under the strain of a deteriorating marriage, he committed suicide by hanging himself on the eve of the band's first tour of the States. His death hurtled him and Joy Division into fame that they could not have otherwise contemplated. For the remaining members the question was whether to continue or to finish; it was under this tragic star that New Order was conceived.

The name immediately caused controversy because of its supposedly fascist over-tones, yet, for the remaining members it was a symbol of their fresh start. The biggest stumbling block, though, for Peter Hook (bass), Bernard Sumner (aka Albrecht, guitar) and Stephen Morris (drums) was Joy Division's towering legacy. Immediately they set to work, and by the late summer of 1980 they had recorded some new demo's and played their first gig (supporting their Factory stable mates, A Certain Ratio). By the end of the year they asked Gillian Gilbert, an old friend, to play keyboards with them. Their first single release (**Ceremony /In A Lonely Place**) was a number previously recorded with Joy Division and so the long shadow of Ian Curtis continued to loom large over their new departures.

Although they continued to garner support from most quarters (mainly because of the JD ghost) their first album, **Movement,** relied heavily on the spirit of their previous work. By this time, they had toured extensively and released a second single **Procession/Everything's Gone Green,** but still the tone of their work trapped them within the boundaries of a morbid death cult. It wasn't until the release of **Temptation,** in

April 1982, that they broke onto a wider market. **Temptation** marked the true beginnings of a New Order (in a literal sense) taking the solid (though occasionally stolid) rhythms of Hook and Morris, and turning them into a compulsive dance floor delight. The move towards a more accessible – and thus a more commercially viable sound – was obvious, unfortunately the band was less than obvious.

Much of Joy Division's reputation had been built on supposition and superstition, grounded as it was on the band's uncooperative stance with the press. This 'hide-go-seek' attitude towards the media continued with New Order and yet another cult was growing; silence was construed as wisdom, privacy as secrecy.

In reality, New Order had a fine sense of the absurd (playing many a prank on unwary journalists) and a sharp Northern wit. Unfortunately they were bound to the grey edifice that had become Factory records and the wilful myopia of press and fans alike. It wasn't until **Blue Monday** stormed the dance floors of a nation that New Order finally came in from the cold.

Blue Monday, in its 12 inch only pressing, was a scorching affirmation of the group's maturity. It nudged its way to the Number 12 slot in April 1983, but

after becoming a crucial Summer anthem, it re-emerged in the charts in September, selling over a million copies world wide, entering the top ten and displacing its follow up (the Arthur Baker produced **Confusion**).

Blue Monday's success was undoubtedly built on its crossover strength; to the old following the band still remained credible and to the new audience they held unknown pleasures. Winning the respect of both the elitist club crowd and the regular pop fan was a magnificent coup. (The single's astonishing return to the top ten was due largely to its popularity in the nightclubs of the mediterranean – a holidaymaker's hit no less!)

Hot on **Blue Monday's** heels came the group's second LP, **Power, Corruption And Lies,** which reached Number Four in the charts and displayed their new spirit and zeal at its fullest. Gone – for the most

part – were the pseudo-Curtis lyrics and in came their enlivened (and enlightened) lines of self-determination and certainty.

Already this year they have seen chart placings with **Thieves Like Us** (released in April) and **Murder** (released in May), and are continuing to build on their new found fame. Although still signed to Factory they seem fully capable of taking on the established bands, most of whom are signed to major labels. (They recently grossed over £100,000 in royalties after Paul Young covered the celebrated Joy Division classic **Love Will Tear Us Apart.**)

It would appear that New Order have finally found their own feet, free from the restraints of the past. They have survived unscathed by their experiences and, most importantly of all, they have won through on their own ground. For New Order it's just beginning.

THE POLICE

● Above:
Andy Summers, Sting
and Stewart Copeland.

For the group who've come closest to challenging the Beatles in terms of all-conquering rock and roll statistics in the last three years, it's no exaggeration to say that the Police would have had difficulty getting themselves arrested for the first two years of their existence – such was the public's lack of interest.

But those two years in the wilderness meant that when the pendulum swung - and kept swinging - their way, the Police were in a better position to control it than most. They'd perfected a style that had become a vitally distinctive trademark and later became the springboard for multi-million selling albums like **Ghost In The Machine** and **Synchronicity.**

In America they are frequently regarded as the ultimate success of the New Wave. But in England, when they first appeared in March 1977 supporting Cherry Vanilla (and acting as her backing band, which was how they got the gig), they were nobody's idea of a New Wave band. They were generally regarded as charlatans, whose previous experience barred them from punk membership.

Stewart Copeland, who conceived the idea of the Police towards the end of 1976 and then set about recruiting the members, had previously been the drummer in Curved Air – the kind of 'progressive' band that was anathema to all true punks.

He couldn't even claim to have created much of a reputation with his only other band. He'd almost been elbowed out of

"Playing with the Police makes you go deeper into your instrument."

ANDY SUMMERS

the studio on his first album with Curved Air and had resorted to writing his own fan mail to the music papers to secure his position in the group. Indeed, about the only positive thing he got out of Curved Air was a love affair with their singer, Sonja Kristina, which has outlasted every other relationship in the Police.

He'd come across Sting in Newcastle, during Curved Air's last tour, singing with a jazz-rock group called Last Exit. He saw *"a young man in an old band — a vibrant force surrounded by fuddy duddies".*

If Stewart had spotted some of Sting's potential, almost nobody else had. Not even Sting. His only attempt to leave home in 1969, to go to college in Coventry, had failed ignominiously and within a month he was back. Since then he'd become a teacher and played with various local bands, writing occasional songs for them.

The only other person who could see star quality in Sting was his wife, actress Frances Tomelty. With their baby boy, they moved down to London early in 1977 in answer to Stewart's call and spent several months sleeping on friends' floors.

The Police's bid for street credibility was their first guitarist, a young Corsican, Flaming Groovies fanatic called Henri

Padovani, who was so steeped in punk ideology that Stewart had to teach him the guitar chords privately before they rehearsed with Sting.

Stewart's single-minded enthusiasm also stretched to writing, recording, packing and distributing their first single – a heavy headlong thrash called **Fall Out** – which sold a creditable 10,000 copies.

But Sting's commitment was wavering without a suitable setting for his burgeoning songwriting, and when Andy Summers, a guitarist who'd already spent 14 years as a sideman with Zoot Money's Big Roll Band, Soft Machine, the

New Animals, Kevin Coyne and Kevin Ayres, asked to join the band, Stewart's astonishment didn't obscure his view of the lifeline – he was about to lose either Sting or Henri.

With the final nail in their credibility coffin hammered in, what gigs the Police could hustle were ignored by press and punters alike. They paid the rent by hiring themselves out to German avant garde composer Eberhard Schoener as musicians and getting bit parts in TV commercials. Wrigley's gum wanted a blond pop group for their advertisement. The Police were happy to oblige.

But within the group, Andy's arrival was paying off. Sting was starting to come up with songs, among them **Roxanne** which was inspired by a wander through the Parisian red light district.

Stewart decided to borrow £2,000 from his elder brother Miles – a manager-promoter who kept suggesting 'proper' bands for Stewart to join – to record an album.

For that money they got Surrey Sound Studio in Leatherhead, a small theatre converted by self-taught producer Nigel Gray, who was looking for business to test out his 16-track equipment.

In January 1978, a year after they'd started, they began recording **Outlandos D'Amour.** Tracks like **Can't Stand Losing You** and **So Lonely** established their

'white' approach to reggae, using the space the rhythms provided to create their own identity and adding sudden bursts of harder Western rock.

But it was **Roxanne** that impressed Miles Copeland, when he dropped by to check on his investment. He put his mouth where some of his money had been and got a no-advance/reasonable royalty deal with A&M.

Even though **Roxanne** got minimal airplay and not many more sales when it was released in April 1978, A&M remained enthusiastic and put out **Can't Stand Losing You** in August, but to no better effect.

They'd been gigging in fits and starts, but it was in America that they got their

"If you can transcend the screaming you can take a generation with you into something else. It's a real challenge."

STING

THE POLICE

THE P OLICE

first sustained bout of touring. They flew over on Freddie Laker's Skytrain to play a month of club dates on the East Coast, on a budget circuit set up by Stewart's other brother Ian, who had an agency in New York.

Roxanne started picking up airplay along the way and even achieved modest chart success. Even better, when they returned to England they suddenly found an audience waiting for them. The singles might not have been hits, but they had spread a message.

Outlandos D'Amour soon recouped its low-budget outlay when it came out in October 1978 – the Police have always been in the supremely fortunate position of never owing their record company a penny – and provided enough to maintain the same principles for their second, **Regatta De Blanc**, which they started recording at Surrey Sound in the Spring of 1979.

This time they had the confidence and awareness to spot their own promise. **Message In A Bottle** and **Walking On The Moon** are prime examples of a band with enough faith in itself to let the songs speak for themselves with simple, stylised arrangements and without any over-embellishment.

But before these gems could get out, **Roxanne** suddenly came good in April 1979, when a determined A&M re-released it. It got to Number 12 and **Outlandos D'Amour** suddenly turned into a chart album.

By the time **Regatta De Blanc** came out in October, the Police buzz was already big enough to sweep it to the top of the charts on the back of **Message In A Bottle**, which was already topping the singles charts.

Sting's songwriting had also done wonders for his photogenic appearance and by the end of the year you couldn't pass a newsstand without seeing his face staring out at you.

Cock-a-hoop, the Police decided to ignore the traditional next move and bypass America, where they'd toured three more times without being able to improve on the first. Instead they toured Australia, Hong Kong, Japan, India and Egypt, the last two blazing a trail into uncharted rock and roll territory.

By the time they got back to England, they were rich enough to become tax exiles and Sting wrote the songs for **Zenyatta Mondatta** closeted away in Eire, while the recording was done in Holland. That helped, but didn't entirely alleviate, the new pressure that now faced the Police. They were expected to deliver the goods, and another hectic touring schedule was being lined up.

Despite being finished hard up against the deadline, **Zenyatta Mondatta**, which came out in autumn 1980, was the album that re-switched America on to the Police, turning triple platinum by the following Spring.

The two hit singles, **Don't Stand So Close To Me** and **De Do Do Do, De Da Da Da**, were perfect three-minute pop songs by Sting, refined by the Police. Elsewhere they expanded the terse rhythmic atmosphere of **The Bed's Too Big Without You** from **Regatta De Blanc** with the eerie, fragmented **Shadows In The Rain** and even made the disco charts with the fierce driving beat of **Voices Inside My Head.**

Each of them was now being hailed as a talented and influential musician in their own right, from Sting's melodious bass and Andy's subtle guitar textures, to Stewart's pioneering reggae crossover drumming technique. Already the cheap imitations were getting record contracts.

By the time America had acquired a taste for the Police, the band were exhausted. The energy that had carried them through the giddy spiral of the last two years was worn out. So they took a break to indulge in individual pursuits – Sting cast himself further into the acting career he'd already begun between Police commitments, while Andy and Stewart immersed themselves in other audio-visual projects.

When they regrouped to record **Ghost In The Machine** later in 1981, they'd had time to assimilate the story so far and concentrated on pleasing themselves, something they'd allowed to slip a little on the last album.

Ghost In The Machine, released at the end of 1981, broke the sequence established by the first three albums by frequently stepping outside the Police's own trade-marks to avoid self-plagarism and also just to see what would happen.

Sting, who'd been reading the works of Arthur Koestler, brought a sustained theme to the lyrics, while the sound developed a thicker, more dissonant texture that was evident even on the singles **Spirits In The Material World** and **Invisible Sun,** where the slow, gentle but incessant message of hope inspired a superb non-political video of children in Northern Ireland, playing normally under grossly abnormal conditions (unfortunately the BBC didn't see it that way and refused to show it).

quenched by experience and acumen.

These virtues may be old-fashioned, but then so is the success that the Police have achieved. It hasn't been done by pandering to adolescent fantasies, but by offering something more substantial that invigorates and challenges you to an opinion. You are not supposed to remain indifferent to the Police.

And in the same old-fashioned way, the Police are still bigger than any of the individuals – Sting included.

Every Little Thing She Does Is Magic took Sting from reggae to calypso, while **Demolition Man** took the group back beyond their own beginnings to being a frantic rock band.

The album's phenomenal success over the ironically more commercially minded **Zenyatta Mondatta** put the Police into the super-league of rock bands. It also took the inevitable toll – Sting and Andy's marriages broke up and there were periodic rumours that the band was about to do the same.

But musically they'd re-awakened their interest and when it came to recording **Synchronicity** at the end of 1982, after another planned rest from each other, they rehearsed it harder than any previous album before going into the studio – now upgraded to Montserrat.

This time Sting used the ideas of Carl Jung for his lyrical framework and the album was a fast-moving succession of songs that walked the fine line between Sting's natural hit-making abilities and the band's often restless character, epitomised by the two singles **Every Breath You Take** and **Wrapped Around Your Finger.**

In sales terms they surpassed themselves yet again and spent a large chunk of 1983 touring round the stadiums of America to audiences up to 70,000 – including Shea Stadium where the Beatles had first triumphed 18 years earlier – carrying around 1000,000 watts of power, 100 speakers, 500 lights and five computers to operate them.

But the chemistry that led to all this is still the same as it was, squeezed into one van with them and all their equipment back in 1977 – a volatile mixture of individual egos, talents and ambitions, dampened but never quite

"The Police are exploiting the multiverse."
STEWART COPELAND

PRETENDERS

In 1979 an American woman with three Englishmen became a major part of the British New Wave invasion. The Pretenders, with lead singer Chrissie Hynde hit the charts with their very first single, **Stop Your Sobbing,** a Ray Davies composition that Chrissie had been in love with ever since she'd heard it performed on The Kinks first album. Although it wasn't a huge hit, it was to mark the beginning of a very successful

for a McLaren group. One of Malcolm's ideas was that Chrissie should not let on that she was a girl, but be disguised as a very effeminate male guitarist. Their material consisted mainly of re-arranged pop standards, but unfortunately they never got further than their rehearsal room and Chrissie was asked to leave. The band, with a few personnel changes, went on to become The Damned, and Chrissie took up session singing, doing

From the 2000 miles video

- **Chrissie Hynde**

career for these four fine musicians.

Chrissie, the band's focal point, was born on September 7, 1951, in Ohio and began her singing career by playing a single gig in her hometown, Akron, with a local group named Sat Sun Mat. In 1974 she came to England and eventually got a job as a freelance journalist with *The New Musical Express.* She wrote articles on several top stars, including David Cassidy, and for a time acted as the paper's singles reviewer.

She left the *NME* after receiving a call from Paris inviting her to join a French band. However, she soon found the language problems working with French musicians were overwhelming, so she packed her bags again and returned to Akron. There, she joined an R & B group, Jack Rabbit, but as fate would have it, they soon broke up, so Chrissie, again out of work, was invited back to Paris to join yet another band, the Frenchies. They also failed to make any impact, so, after six months, she decided to try her luck again in London, where the punk scene was just beginning to happen.

Malcolm McLaren, whose boutique she'd worked in when she'd first come to England, heard she was back in town and invited her to join a band called Masters of the Backside – a typical name

back up vocals for such artists as Johnny Moped, Nick Lowe and Chris Spedding.

During this period she spent all her time writing songs and making demo tapes with a variety of musician friends. Then she was introduced to the head of A & R at Anchor records, Dave Hill, who at this time was in the throes of setting up his own label, Real records, which would be financed and marketed by Anchor. He was very impressed with some of her demos and introduced her to drummer Gas Wild, advancing them some money

to get a band together. Gas brought in a bass player who was an old school friend, Pete Farndon. They spent time working together, but Gas didn't suit their style and soon left.

After days of auditions for guitarists and drummers contacted through ads in the music papers, Pete brought in an ex-girlfriend's brother named Jimmy Honeyman-Scott, who'd given up guitar to work in a music shop in Hereford. Still

short of a drummer, they found a session player, Gerry Mackleduff, whom they had to pay a fee for all rehearsals and sessions. Together they went into the studios and recorded several numbers, including two of Chrissie's own compositions, **Precious** and **The Wait,** together with **Stop Your Sobbing.**

Chrissie was so enthusiastic over the session that she called Nick Lowe straight away and talked him into listening to the tape. What he didn't know was that she was making the call from a phone box in the next street and she arrived on his doorstep two minutes later. Nick listened to the tape, and hated the arrangement of **Stop Your Sobbing,** but saw the potential in the track and in Chrissie's voice.

He was in the middle of producing an album with Elvis Costello, but arranged to use some of the studio time to re-record two tracks with the Pretenders, which were completed in a day. They were all so happy with the result of the session, that they forgot to record backing vocals on **Sobbing,** so Nick Lowe ended up doing most of them himself.

The single was released by Real records, giving the label its first chart entry and was hailed as one of the best first records by a new band for many years. Their second single, **Kid,** written by Chrissie Hynde and produced by Chris Thomas, also became a small hit, reaching one place higher in the charts than their first single.

But it was their third single, **Brass In Pocket** taken from the album they were working on with Thomas, that gave them their first Number One hit in Britain and Australia. The album was released at the beginning of 1980 and entered the charts at Number One.

The Pretenders spent most of that year touring and the release of another single from their first album gave them another top ten hit with **Talk Of The Town.**

The next year they released their second album **Pretenders II,** which they followed up with another world tour. Unfortunately it was during this tour that the band's drummer, Martin Chambers, sustained a hand injury and the US gigs had to be postponed. When they did eventually take place, it was to be the last time the original line up of the Pretenders played together.

In 1982 Pete Farndon quit over internal politics and soon afterwards James Honeyman-Scott died of a cocaine overdose. These events caused the remainder of the band to go to pieces, and for several months they ceased working. Then Chrissie, expecting a baby by Ray Davies, got together again with Chambers and called on the help of Billy Bremner, guitarist with Rockpile, to record **Back On The Chain Gang.** This was dedicated to Honeyman-Scott and became another top twenty hit on both sides of the Atlantic.

In January 1983 Chrissie gave birth to a baby girl, but three months later tragedy struck again when Pete Farndon suddenly died of heart failure, brought on by drug abuse, just after getting a new band of his own together. The Pretenders, however, with a new line up which included Malcolm Foster on bass guitar and Robbie McIntosh on guitar, continued having success and were back in the charts with a Christmas hit **2000 Miles.** The first album with the new line up was released in March 1984, again produced by Chris Thomas and called **Learning To Crawl.** Another hit single **Thin Line Between Love And Hate,** originally a soul hit in the States for the Persuaders, resulted.

Their fifth album, recorded in Abba's studios in Sweden with producer Steve Lillywhite, will be followed by another world tour. On a happy note, the American leg of the tour is with Simple Minds whose lead singer, Jim Kerr, married Chrissie Hynde after a whirlwind romance, which was undoubtedly the best kept secret in the music business in 1984.

PRETENDERS

● The original line-up: Pete Farndon, Martin Chambers, Chrissie Hynde and James Honeyman-Scott.

Lionel Richie

Lionel Richie, almost overnight, has become the world's top singing sex symbol. Without anybody really noticing, he's become one of the most successful singer/songwriters of all-time. Yet he still remains an affable enigma.

The fact is that the mass world hysteria about Michael Jackson over the last two years has robbed Richie of much acclaim. But it's a position Lionel is used to. Even at the beginning of his music career with the Commodores at Motown, Richie and his chums were in the shadows of the Jackson 5. Rumour even has it that the Commodores used to play behind the curtains to 'beef up' the Jackson 5's stage sound. While it's probably just another of the many apocryphal stores surrounding Michael Jackson, there is no doubt that the Commodores were an almost permanent fixture on Jackson 5 tours.

It was apt that both bands should have been together. They both represented important watersheds in the history of their Tamla Motown home.

The Jackson 5 were to prove the last glorious gasp of the Tamla Motown hit machine - the assembly line system that

This barely contained cacophony influenced everybody. The great bulk of disco and funk today, simply work off variations of Sly and the Family Stone's innovations. No one has really got past them.

The effervescence of the Jackson 5 can be traced directly to Sly Stone. The influence was widespread and many bands joined the new order.

One such band was The Jays from Tuskagee, Alabama. They came together in 1968 at college. Their first gig was prompted by demands from their school seniors - who promptly showered them with water-filled balloons and raucous laughter!

The basic line-up of Lionel Richie (tenor saxaphone), William King (trumpet), Thomas McClary (lead guitar) and Milan Williams (keyboards, drums and guitar), was established. A couple of changes saw Walter 'Clyde' Orange (drums and vocals) and Ronald LaPread (bass and trumpet), complete the formation.

Most of the band still live there now, having married girlfriends from those schooldays.

Lionel was brought up in middle class

"Gran felt it would give me a little culture and stop me becoming a hoodlum."

had paid such rich dividends throughout the sixties.

Michael Jackson's astonishing debut with his brothers on **I Want You Back** was the peak of the corporate workings of the world's largest black owned business. The full weight of the Motown heritage - so successful with acts like Diana Ross and the Supremes, Four Tops, Marvin Gaye, Temptations and Stevie Wonder - was ingrained into the Jackson 5 in the year between their signing for the label and their debut in December 1969.

The Commodores were the first stirrings of the new order - the way Motown boss, Berry Gordy, knew he had to go to successfully traverse the seventies.

By the end of the 1960's the more militant aspects of black power in America had given way to the less violent, but deeply felt notion of black pride. Pride in achievement, enjoyment of brotherhood, a feeling of common purpose and shared triumphs.

It was Sly and the Family Stone, the multi-racial band who came to prominence with **Dance To The Music** in 1968, who captured the celebratory mood. And more importantly, sold it to the mass rock audience.

That debut ended the domination of Motown, Stax and Atlantic; sweet soul was no more.

Before Sly, soul records had been conceived as vocal vehicles. Rock bands changed that; in the music of San Francisco, the vocals were an afterthought. **Dance To The Music** joined them, brutally - the voice and the music didn't achieve equality, they fought for space, right on the disc.

America. He'd intended to be a lawyer until the Commodores. He was born on the campus and learned classical music from his grandmother, the Institute's choir director.

"She was darn good," recalls Lionel, *"and those early lessons provided the background to my writing success.*

"Gran felt it would give me a little culture and stop me becoming a hoodlum."

What Gran didn't realise was that her grandson had an incredible memory. She was convinced that she had taught him to read music, until one day during a lesson she turned over one sheet too many on the music sheet he was playing from. Young Lionel continued to play the correct part. He was memorising Bach and Beethoven and fooling Gran all the time.

Lionel had other family influences. His Uncle Bertram was an arranger for Duke Ellington, so Lionel was exposed to jazz. He was from a church-going family, so gospel was another influence. The radio offered cosmopolitan rock and singer-songwriter soft-rock types, and, at the other end of the dial, country and western. Lionel soaked up these influences reasonably indiscriminately, but with a special emphasis on every genre of emotive balladry.

But the era was post-Sly Stone and everybody was churning out the tougher street funk style. The Jays had played small clubs in New York and even got bookings in Canada and Europe.

In 1970 they were offered the support slot to the Jackson 5 tour. It was this that led them to a record contract with

Lionel Richie

Motown in 1972. Motown were looking to them to ease their way into the new age of soul. One that meant groups (they'd already failed with Rare Earth).

Selecting 'commodore' from a dictionary at random, Motown set the group on course with their debut single and album **Machine Gun** in 1974. The single was a hard rocking synthesiser instrumental in the disco funk mould. It was a smash worldwide and earned them gold singles and albums.

Obviously, because it was Motown, the Commodores scored because their funk was streamlined and clean in comparison to, say, the Ohio Players or Kool And The Gang. The second album **Caught In The Act** also went gold. They went from strength to strength over the next few years, rarely stepping outside their dance-orientated appeal. Then came **Zoom,** their 1977 album. It contained the lush ballad **Easy** - written by Lionel Richie – and it pinpointed that the pen of Lionel Richie was going to be their most successful direction over the next few years.

> **"I found out how to get a song on the group album guaranteed – bring in a slow one. That's how I got to writing slow songs."**

He says: *"The only reason I wrote all these ballads for the Commodores was because everybody brought in 10 songs apiece and the problem was that everybody brought in 10 fast songs. I found out how to get a song on the group album guaranteed — bring in a slow one. That's how I got to writing slow songs."*

Another incident made him settle on the genre. He was nominated for a Grammy – the musical Oscars – in the Best R & B category. He couldn't understand it when Britain's Leo Sayer scooped the award with **When I Need You.** He didn't even realise it was an R & B single. It was then that Richie realised that the general public were just looking for different ways of saying *"I love you"* to each other. It also occured to him that ballads remain in the memory far longer than the faster records of any act.

With this in mind, Lionel Richie set about refining his craft. He was only too successful. The Commodores' wish to be regarded as 'the black Beatles' came closer to fruition as Richie buckled down.

In 1978 Richie's **Three Times A Lady** scored a Number One hit in virtually every country. It started a run that has continued to this day. Richie has written an American Number One in every year since.

In 1979 it was **Still.** In 1980 it was **Lady** for Kenny Rogers – with whom he now shares management. In 1981 it was his **Endless Love** duet with Diana Ross. He

● Lionel Richie and his wife Brenda

also earned the impressive distinction of being the first person in Billboard chart history to appear in one guise or another with three songs in the top 10. He was songwriter for **Endless Love** (nine weeks at Number One and 10th best seller of all time in the USA), performer on the Commodores' **Lady (You Bring Me Up)**, as well as producer with Kenny Rogers' **I Don't Need You.**

It was obvious that Motown had a hot property on their hands and pressure would be put on Richie to become a solo artist. He split from the Commodores in 1982.

"With all that going on, it wouldn't have been fair to the Commodores or to myself to stay with them," he said. *"This business is like a great big toy shop and there are so many departments I want to look in on. To begin with, there is my singing and songwriting as a solo artist, then there's the movie industry, Broadway, producing other artists and there's publishing, which sees me with a businessman's hat on during the occasional afternoon."* (He has attempted to major in Economics and Accountancy.)

Endless Love was later nominated for no less than seven Grammy awards and an Oscar.

Lionel's first solo album was released in 1982. It was named after the artist and kept up his record of having a US Number One hit single every year with **Truly.** Another worldwide smash.

While critics love their soul men to occupy comfortable categories, and stay there, Richie has been a frustrating man to pin down. He has always considered himself an entertainer, rather than a soul singer. His songs don't have much blues or afro in them and he's only paid the merest attention to white rock.

He's a funk band member whose forte is ballads; a black man who writes not just country songs, but what one writer described as "countrypolitan ones"; his writing is full of sophisticated references to jazz, Stevie Wonder and Marvin Gaye.

He operates in a tradition that ranges from Nat 'King' Cole to George Benson. It's a tradition that receives scant appraisal from the media. Crooners have always been an integral part of the soul spectrum – if the least publicised of its branches.

In only three years Richie has become a multi-millionaire. Like Stevie Wonder's, the Richie talent is never more evident than when it is veering towards the sentimental.

It's this ability to be deeply expressive about pledging undying sexual and spiritual fidelity, that has made him one of the most popular artists of the past six years. Although the Commodores refined funk opened the door to people like Rick James and George Clinton's madhouse, and they had more range than any other

> **"The priesthood was a little too heavy for me, the wrong road. But my mission is to touch lives."**

band of their genre; it is Richie that dominates any appraisal. When Motown released a Commodores' Anthology in mid-1983, Richie wrote or co-wrote 14 of its 20 songs and all but one song on its final three sides.

He has become the Don Juan of the charts. The shy, man whose every word hangs heavy with romance. The tender charmer who makes every moment of love seem like the last time the listener is going to be kissed, caressed or made love to by the lover of their dreams.

Lady alone made Lionel Richie a million dollars, and earned him a share in the cosmetics range named after the song. He has grand pianos in each of his three homes, and in the homes of any relatives

he may visit, in case inspiration strikes. He regularly wakes up in the middle of the night, writes down some notes, going back to sleep and not remembering writing anything until he sees the scraps of paper next morning.

"It's a gift," he says. *"I can't understand how everybody else don't hear songs floating around in their heads like I do. All I have to do is sit down at a piano and copy them."*

His tone suggest divine guidance.

"I always knew I was going to be in the service business," he says. *"The priesthood was a little too heavy for me, the wrong road. But my mission is to touch lives."*

1983 saw the release of Richie's second solo album **Can't Slow Down.** The first single **All Night Long (All Night)** was a worldwide smash of immense proportions. It was universally adored by audience and critics alike for its afro swagger and infectious exuberance. It was his 1983 US Number One. His US 1984 Number One was **Hello** - aided by one of the most cloyingly sentimental videos of all time - Richie produced a monster single. It became Motown's biggest ever single in Britain with over 800,000 copies sold and spending six weeks at Number One.

The album has sold around 10 million to date and a worldwide tour — which includes Richie singing a duet with Diana Ross on a lifesize video on **Endless Love** – is expected to increase that figure substantially.

It is clear that the star of Lionel Richie has still some way to rise. And as long as there are people who prefer to hear someone else say *"I love you"* for them, then Richie is in business.

Whether he'll feel the need to break out of the basic love situation lyrically – as he did to great success on **All Night Long (All Night)** – remains to be seen.

Lionel Richie

SADE

The hospital on the university campus in Ibadan, Nigeria, is not a common birthplace for pop stars. But it was there in 1960 that Helen Fola-Sade Adu gave her first screams.

Twenty four years later and young Sade (pronounced Sharday) is the name to drop. Her cool, androgynous beauty and smoky late night voice have led to immediate comparisons with older torch singers like Billie Holliday or Edith Piaf.

And perhaps because it is indicative of a new musical sophistication in the pop charts, she manages to hit popular appeal and critical plaudits in the same breath.

The product of a mixed marriage between an English nurse, Ann, and a Nigerian Economics lecturer, Bisi, that sadly never made it over the long term, Sade has inherited the best aspects of their blood lines. Added to her natural looks and bouncing personality, she has added an extra element. That of the untouchable.

Sade had conceived of her image long before the general public caught up with her. She pulls back her hair into a severe – if false – plait, that somehow narrows her eyes into a hint of the Orient. Her clothes are functional and sombre, vaguely masculine tunics, trousers to the mid-shin, macs with militaristic, padded shoulders. It is all slightly forbidden, slightly gender teasing. Sade should star in recruiting posters for the North Korean Army, except she sings rather than shoots.

Mrs Ann Adu returned to England when Sade was four and her brother, Banji, seven. They settled in a tiny hamlet in Essex.

"We came back here with no money." Sade recalls, "My first memory is of snow, which I had never seen before, and how very cold it was in the winter of 1963."

Her aunt had also married a Nigerian, and her mother was a staunch Labour supporter, so Sade grew up without understanding the horror of racial prejudice. She remembers being surprised at the sight of this big black man in a pinstripe suit standing in the village street. It was her father on his way to lecture in Yale University.

Such things changed, though, in her 12th year. Her mother remarried an East End butcher, rejoicing in the unlikely and unfortunate name of Marquis (Sade Marquis – get it?) and the family moved to Clacton-on-Sea. Joining the secondary school there was something of a revelation. Other kids were not too crazy about her colouring.

"You don't stay in Clacton when you leave school," she says with a wry grin. "Unless you stay for life. Half the

population is over 65, the other 50 per cent are poodles. If I ever really want to make any money, I'll just open a poodle parlour in Clacton."

Nor was Clacton a musical Mecca. Her soul/jazz preferences were too weird for the punks and heavy metal bikers who made up the local teen crowd. From a very early age she had snaffled a couple of her mother's albums and loudly played them to death (**Dinah Washington's Greatest Hits** and Frank Sinatra singing with Count Basie). Throughout her teen years she cultivated a taste for Ray Charles, Aretha Franklin, Billie Holliday, Nina Simone and jazz greats like John Coltrane and Roland Kirk.

Life with Mr Marquis was not too wonderful, so as soon as possible Sade upped and left for London, where she entered the prestigious St Martin's College Of Art to study fashion design. St Martin's has always been painfully trendy, but this was the era of the New Romantics. It was chic once more to wear outrageous clothes. Probably as a reaction, Sade stuck to the severe functional negatives of black.

Those were the days when it was still enough just to have an image, being asked to join a band was a natural

Having convinced Pride of the error of their ways, Sade enlisted herself as second back up singer. The band were a very loose seven piece funk outfit, fun in the clubs, but lacking in the consummate professionalism and musical ability that characterises their American funk counterparts.

Tiring of the same material, Sade began to write her own songs. In a bloodless coup, accompanied by Pride men Paul Denman on bass, Paul Cook on drums, Stewart Matthewman on guitar and saxophone, and Andrew Hale on piano, they began to play their own little set.

Julie London's endearing ballad **Cry Me A River** (before the Neasden Beehive queen Mari Wilson) and other jazz and soul classics were rendered sensitively and respectfully. Sade, the group, became more popular than Pride with the audience.

A recording contract with Epic led to studio sessions with Robin Millar, a 32-year-old Cambridge graduate of music. Millar, who has been going blind since the age of six with the degenerative disease of *retinus pigmentosa,* bases his operations in his own Powerplant studio in Willesden and has been dubbed the 'acoustic Trevor Horn' because of his

Holliday comparison. A snapped line *"I'm not a junkie like her"* has lost her a few friends along the way, but Miss Adu takes that in her stride. As would anyone who suffered the indignities of production line modelling to pay for rehearsals in the early days of the band.

Her second single, the directly political **When Am I Gonna Make A Living**, stalled at the bottom end of the top 40. Written on the back of a soggy envelope when she *"was walking from Turnpike Lane tube station. It was pouring and I was soaking wet, pissed off and miserable",* the song has become the anthem for the stage set.

Her first album **Diamond Life,** released in July, confirmed Sade's steady progress towards the top. Full of strong sensitive songs that highlight her voice – which even she will admit is not the strongest around – it flatters, but does not deceive.

She lives in a rundown flat in Haringey, North London, with her journalist boy-friend Robert Elms. Cynics say that Elms is Sade's *eminence grise,* that he has moulded her into his image. There may be some truth there, for Elms was the original chronicler of the New Romantic movement, virtually singlehanded he elevated Spandau Ballet onto the early

corollary of the look. So it was with Sade.

"I always used to sing around the house even when I was big, I wasn't self-conscious about it. But I never thought of joining a band until the manager of Pride asked me to sing back up.

"Actually when I auditioned for them, they rejected me. I was so shocked. It wasn't a question of never failing at anything, but all the things I'd really wanted to do till then I'd done."

productions with such groups as Everything But The Girl, Working Week and Pale Fountains.

The very first flower in his garden is Sade. Her first single, the delightful **Your Love Is King** charmed its way into the top ten, drawing admiring comparisons to Billie Holliday and drooling references from besotted male jounalists – and a few female ones as well.

Sade has never been happy with the

steps of the rock ladder. However no one can groom Sade into her greatest asset: her natural charm.

There is a legend, probably apocryphal, circulating the music business about her record company PR and a national newspaper journalist.

"I know she's pretty," said the journalist, *"But can she talk? Is she interesting?"* *"Interesting?"* replied the PR, *"I'd like to marry her!"*

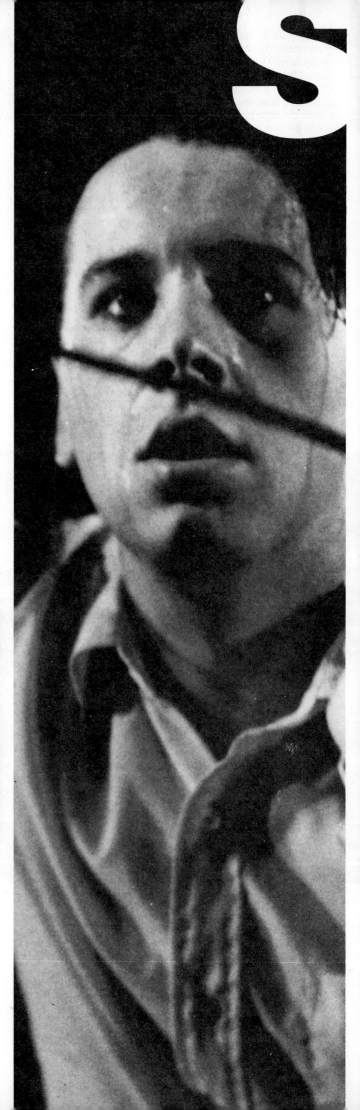

By the bitterest of ironies, Simple Minds' career has frequently been retarded by their own excellence. They are undoubtedly one of the most sophisticated and imaginative units currently operating, and have succeeded in proving time and again, that their most valuable qualities have a habit of flying over the heads of the public at large. Their latest LP, **Sparkle In The Rain,** was an attempt to seize some of rock's middle ground, while there is evidence to suggest that the Minds are trying to introduce a more crowd-pleasing element into their live shows. Results so far have proved inconclusive.

Jim Kerr (born July 9, 1959), vocalist and frontman, was originally in a primitive Glasgow semi-punk band, rather charmingly called Johnny And The Self Abusers. This outfit also included Kerr's schoolfriends Brian McGee and Charlie Burchill (born November 27, 1959) on drums and guitar respectively, and as the Self Abusers imploded, these three recruited bassman Derek Forbes (born June 27, 1956) and keyboard specialist Mick MacNeil (born July 20, 1958) to form Simple Minds.

Brimming with energy, the Minds swiftly hitched up with Edinburgh record shop mogul Bruce Findlay, who became their manager and signed them to his own Zoom label, which was distributed by Arista. By the end of 1979, they'd already released two LPs. First came the quirky, imaginative, but somewhat derivative **Life In A Day,** featuring the celebrated **Chelsea Girl** (the hit single that never was). It was followed by **Real To Real Cacophony,** an album split about equally between weird noises and

● Jim Kerr

ominous hard rock, such as **Premonition.** So far, observers were having difficulty in deciding whether Simple Minds was merely a compilation of influences (Roxy Music, Magazine, Doctors Of Madness, Genesis and the Velvet Underground) or genuine new force.

Proof arrived with album number three, 1980's remarkable **Empires And Dance.** Entirely different from anything they'd done before, **Empires** was a riveting electronic travelogue rumbling with doubt and lit by uncomfortable flashes of revelation. Suddenly, Simple Minds had crystallised a focus and direction, and it was more than anyone could have anticipated. Songs like **I Travel** and **Celebrate** used insistently repeating rhythms to generate enormous power, and it seemed that German electronic groups, like Kraftwerk, had exerted a considerable influence – the Minds had, after all, recently played numerous dates throughout Europe. In keeping with the stark, mechanical modernity of the music, Simple Minds onstage were now polarised in black and white, with Kerr (black hair, white shirt) enacting his fractured lyrics like some diabolic princeling. They still couldn't get a hit single, though.

A complete breakdown of communication with Arista found Simple Minds arranging a transfer to Virgin, where they hitched up with old hippie guitarist Steve Hillage as producer to record the double set of **Sons And Fascination/Sister Feelings Call.** The sessions overran both their allotted time and their budget, and there were some filler tracks. But songs like **Seeing Out The Angel, Love Song, In Trance As Mission** and **The American** built on the sort of repeating rhythms demonstrated on **Empires,** while introducing unexpected new dimensions of emotion. Simple Minds had invented a kind of symphonic funk. Meanwhile, drummer Brian McGee had succumbed to the stress of almost constant touring and quit.

When **Promised You A Miracle** at last gave the Minds a hit single in the spring of 1982, they'd probably given up hoping it could ever happen. It marked the start of their most fruitful phase so far, since by then they'd started to amass ideas for what would become **New Gold Dream (81-82-83-84),** the album which would mark the high tide of their creativity to date.

There are a few criticisms applicable to **Dream** – the record was cut too quietly, for some reason, while producer Pete Walsh didn't capture the tough cutting edge the Minds could deliver on a good night onstage. But on the other hand, most of the songs were shot through with a poignancy and melodic grace rarely matched in rock music.

Someone Somewhere In Summertime, Big Sleep, Hunter And The Hunted . . . all of them were songs of great beauty and enormous sadness, simultaneously celebrations of the intricacies Simple Minds were now capable of, while also requiems for something coming to a close.

The departure of drummer McGee had resulted in a string of temporary stand-ins before former session man Mel Gaynor (born May 29, 1960) was offered the job in late '82. He's been there ever since. Gaynor's integration into Simple Minds coincided with what can now be seen as a decision to aim squarely for the fat heart of the mainstream rock audience.

After some dithering over Alex Sadkin, they settled on the ubiquitous Steve Lillywhite as their new producer. He'd already made three albums with U2, as well as Big Country's **The Crossing,** when he began working with the Minds – it seemed as though they'd decided to throw in their lot with the so-called New Rock movement currently being built up by the music press. This was disappointing, since Simple Minds had never before needed to declare any allegiance to anyone but themselves.

Still, the resulting **Sparkle In The Rain** set was a good record by anybody's standards. **Up On The Catwalk, The Book Of Brilliant Things** and especially **Speed Your Love To Me** were all muscular and memorable, while **Kick Inside** generated an animal power new for the band and **Waterfront** had already proved itself as a hit single. But at the same time something had been lost. Maybe it was because Mel Gaynor's massive machine-gun percussion overshadowed the interplay between Burchill's guitar and MacNeil's artful keyboards, or maybe it was just that they suddenly sounded like other rock groups. **Sparkle** had power and presence, but the magic had been sold short. Nevertheless it entered the British charts at Number One early in 1984.

Then strange things began to happen around Simple Minds. Kerr fell ill during a British tour – again the result of endless days on the road – then out of the blue

came the news that he'd married Chrissie Hynde of The Pretenders in New York. Was this unexpected union between the charismatic Kerr and the leather-clad rock queen from a different generation a hint of the way things would go?

The London dates which Simple Minds played soon afterwards were, for whatever reason, a heady mixture of tragedy and farce. The stage curtains opened to reveal Kerr perched none too steadily up a pole, and throughout the set he hectored the audience with grandiose announcements and shouts of *"Up!"* and *"Higher!"* He seemed to have fallen under the spell of U2's Bono, a man much better suited to the dramatic gesture – Kerr simply looked like a man trying on an ill-fitting new personality in public. Worst of all, the band collectively played as though auditioning for a spot on the Des O'Conner Show, devoid of their usual subtlety and grace.

The reasons for this abrupt change of identity could only be guessed at, though the best bet seemed to be ambitions in the American market. The Minds had quite possibly become tired of being a critics' band, who never broke through to the larger audiences they desired. Nonetheless it would be a shame if they sacrificed all their unique qualities in exchange for mass appeal. Only time will tell.

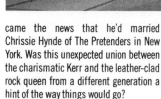

▶SIMPLE MINDS

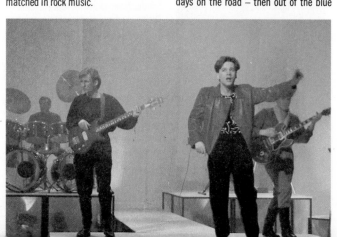

● Johnny Marr

● Morrissey

●Andy Rourke

If any one band has re-vitalised the generally vapid pop-scene of 1984, it is that charming Mancunian quartet The Smiths. Armed with little more than a quiver of fresh, simple songs and a fist full of flowers, they have won over a public increasingly bored with artists (sic) of slim potential and fatuous talent. This is a point that Morrissey, their lead singer and songwriter, insists on pushing home to the media – convinced as he is of the band's immeasurable importance. Oddly enough, and in spite of his cultured arrogance, the country seems to have fallen in love with this disarmingly honest individual. It could just be that he is telling the truth when he claims that The Smiths are more important than The Police.

The origins of The Smiths lay in an early meeting between the then Stephen Morrissey (born May 22, 1959) and the band's guitarist and tunesmith, Johnny Marr (born October 31, 1963). Marr, who was 14 at the time, had heard of Morrissey from a couple of his older musical acquaintances and although little came of their first meeting it left a lasting impression on the pair, so much so that four years later Marr could still remember Morrissey's early lyrics. And then came the band. With Andy Rourke (born January 17, 1964) on bass and Mike Joyce (born June 1, 1963) on drums, they played their first gig at The Ritz in Manchester on October 4, 1982, an altogether inauspicious start. But within the space of seven gigs they had attracted a loyal following and a welter of interest from major record companies. Yet it was the small independent set-up, Rough Trade, that signed The Smiths in the face of numerous six-figure offers.

For the band all of this was part and parcel of a well conceived plan; each step was to be taken in their own time and every move had to be surefooted and worthwhile. For Morrissey it was the advent of all he wanted.

Whilst most people spent their youth out

good song and a good singer. With Morrissey at his side he envisaged a partnership of classic dimensions, such as Lieber & Stoller once shared.

Hand in Glove the first, and self-produced, single by The Smiths proved the possibilities and is still regarded by many as their finest song. For Morrissey, it was the most important song in the world (of course!). And, odd though it may sound, he has often said that his entire life was a preparation for that song.

Almost immediately The Smiths were

raised to the same cult level occupied by bands such as Echo And The Bunnymen and U2. Most notably they were voted Best New Act by the readership of *The New Musical Express*.

This Charming Man, though, was the first single to make a mark in the charts, staying as it did for 18 weeks and reaching Number 25. Morrissey, in his loose shirts and baggy jeans, was suddenly elevated to star ranking and, clutching his ubiquitous bunch of flowers to his chest, he was to be seen everywhere. **What Difference Does It Make** rose to Number 12 and their first British tour (which proceeded in spite of Morrissey's illness) was a sell-out affair along the lines of the Chelsea Flower Show.

Quite why this pale and frail looking creature created such a stir could be seen on The Smiths' debut album **The Smiths.** His lyrics re-defined and re-evaluated archaic yet honest words. His references were impeccable. It was if single-handedly he were refreshing the charts with some eccentricity, some character of *worth*.

Whilst all around seemed content in making travelogue-style videos for their songs, The Smiths refused to make even the simplest. But by way of a novelty, they asked Sandie Shaw to sing **Hand In Glove** as a single. For some it was the return to some lost hippy nostalgia (and The Smith's critics continue to call them revivalists), but for Morrissey it was another dream realised.

Heaven Knows I'm Miserable Now, their fourth single, reached Number 10 and ensured them another *Top Of The Pops* appearance – this time with Morrissey, flowers in pocket, kitted out with NHS specs and a hearing aid. Why such an odd character, a pronounced celibate (and thus more androgynous than a thousand Boy Georges – no one's quite sure which way Morrissey swings) and a profoundly retiring man should accrue so much importance in such a

THE SMITH

● Mike Joyce

and about, Morrissey had spent his adolescence in a self-imposed solitary confinement, spurning all worldly delights and dilemmas.

If anything it was this isolation that spurred Morrissey to write, surrounded as he was by nothing but books and a selection of singles from the sixties. And it was this loneliness from which he crafted the Smith's lyrical and spiritual base. Marr, meanwhile, had played in various groups in the Manchester area, but he felt that the main body of his work – simple, melodic tunes – remained without the necessary compliment of a

short space of time is a puzzle. But one thing is for sure; in less than a year The Smiths have forged a resilient beauty. Their candour and confidence has blossomed into the most melodic of spiritual sounds.

There is a rawness in their music that belies their musical age; a fresh, ethereal ability that captures more than just the routine of 'making' good songs. In a great Smith's song there is an over view that simply towers above the congregating mortals in the pop-forum. And for that reason alone, The Smiths are possibly more important than The Police.

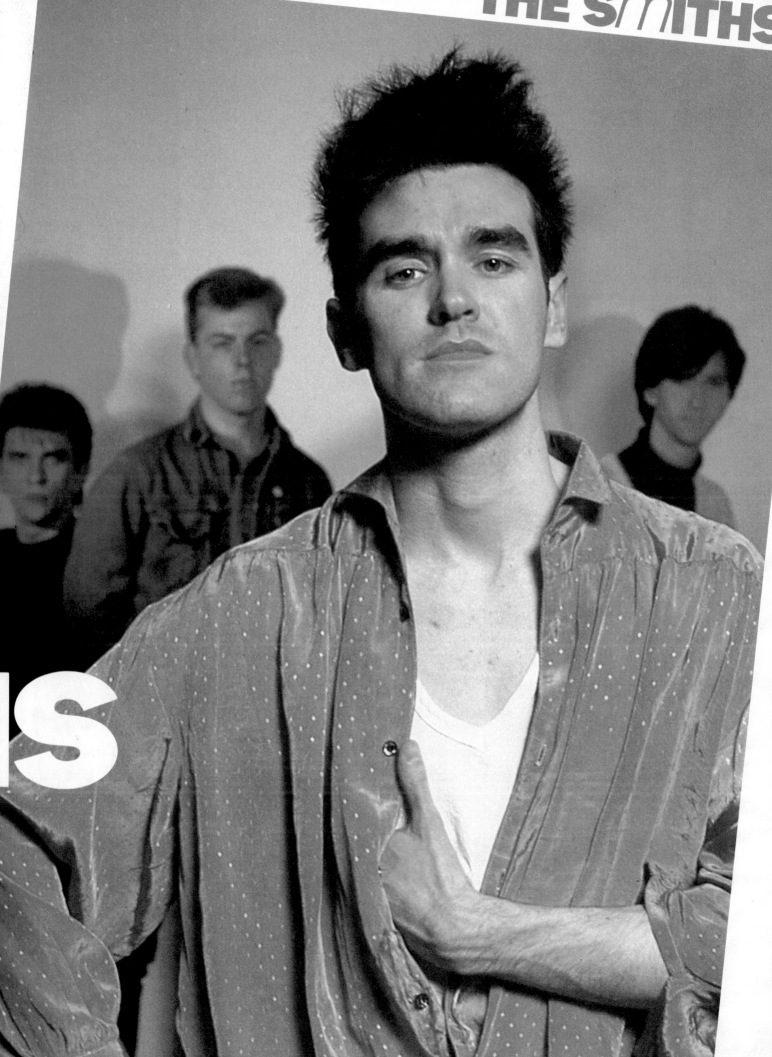

THE SMITHS

IS

London,1979. It was a curious year in the history of the great rock'n'roll swindle. Johnny Rotten had deserted the Sex Pistols, Sid Vicious was dead, and so, to all intents and purposes, was punk. Looking back, it seems like it happened overnight: quite suddenly, like a breath of fresh spring air out of the putrid destruction that was punk, came a movement known as the New Romantics, championed by a hitherto unheard-of band called Spandau Ballet.

Was it all such a happy accident? Not so, sneer the cynics, who recognised immediately what manager Steve Dagger was attempting to do – attract attention to your band by making them as different as you can from the current scene, in this case, punk rock. A while later, when the consumer has caught on, tell the music journalists you were only ever mirroring the tastes of your audiences, thus flattering their egos and nurturing their support. Once they are hooked, you can change your image as often as you like.

That five North London lads of limited education and resources have earned recognition all over the world in their field is an achievement in itself, especially when you consider their grey and humble council-estate beginnings. 1959 saw the arrival of Gary James Kemp (October 16) and John Keeble (July 6). 1960, of Anthony Patrick Hadley (June 2) and Steve Norman (March 25). In 1961 came Gary's brother Martin (October 10). They all attended Owens Grammar School in Islington.

Tony spent his spare time developing those now-famous crooning tones to his mother's record collection, and started winning talent contests when he was 14; his specialities were peculiarly operatic renditions of **With A Little Help From My Friends** and **You Are The Sunshine Of My Life.**

Gary received an appropriate 11th birthday present from his parents – his first guitar. He quickly became a self-taught strummer, and has been writing songs ever since.

Martin, once torn between the two obvious escape routes for a working class kid – pop music and football – originally donned boots for Arsenal schoolboys. His prospects looked good, but his heart was elsewhere. When he was nine, he and elder brother Gary began attending Anna Scher's Children's Theatre in Barnsbury Road, Islington, a respected acting school run by a school-teacher at ten pence per child per session. For Martin, always the best-looking Kemp, it led to minor television roles in the likes of *Play for Today* and *Jackanory*. It also helped him conquer his shyness and develop a taste for showmanship. But he had never touched a musical instrument in his life.

John Keeble quickly became as familiar with a drumkit as with the under-bonnet workings of a clapped-out Cortina, but Steve Norman had never been near a bongo, nor even a saxophone, when the embryonic Spandau emerged from school, joined the ever-growing dole queue and set about acquiring the finer points of posturing and posing which would stand them in good stead around the London clubs.

"The search for the good life is what many working-class kids are about" explains Gary, he of the loudest voice. *"They don't like work, they want to enjoy themselves and look good and be important. That's the kind of lifestyle we grew up with."*

In the late seventies, for the likes of this bunch of North London soulboys, clubs such as Global Village in Charing Cross, Chaguaramas in Covent Garden and Billy's in Dean Street were the places to be seen. At first, it was funk and American disco which captured their imagination. Then along came punk, and the soul movement went underground. A unique brand of self-styled exclusivity set in.

Former Berwick Street barrow-boy

turned LSE Economics student Steve Dagger remembers Rusty Egan as the most creative DJ of the era, mixing the likes of Bowie, Roxy, Kraftwerk and the Human League with seventies soul and getting away with it. Following the example, other clubs in the same vein sprang up. Perhaps the most important of them all was Blitz in Covent Garden, never likely to experience such joyful hedonistic days again. The Blitz Kids were born.

"If a record company had had the suss to come along and sign up the entire contents of the Blitz Club", recalls Steve Dagger, "they would now have about 80 per cent of acts featuring in the British charts — and more besides. The doorman was Steve Strange and the disc jockey was Rusty Egan (poached from Billy's), both of Visage. The cloakroom attendant was Culture Club's Boy George, and the guy who collected the glasses was Marilyn. The customers included the likes of Ultravox, Siouxsie and the Banshees, Haysi Fantaysi, Animal Nite-life, Blue Rondo and Spandau Ballet — who by the turn of the decade had already formed into a group. As well as musicians, the club had everything you need for a major pop culture explosion — graphic artists, embryonic journalists, fashion designers — everything, in fact, except professional management. That's where I stepped in."

Realising that you couldn't stage a Spandau Ballet gig at the Marquee — they would probably have been stoned off by the club's regulars, and Spandau fans would not have been seen dead there — Dagger set about finding a way to present what was quickly becoming an underground cult group. Meanwhile, the media began to pick up on these the forerunners of the New Romantics,

● Gary Kemp, John Keeble, Tony Hadley, Steve Norman. and Martin Kemp

SPANDAU BALLET

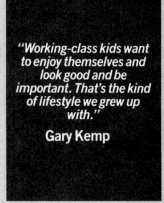

bedecked in tartan and frills. In the summer of 1980, Janet Street-Porter filmed a half-hour television documentary on the Blitz Kids phenomenon, which included a rare appearance by the band at the Scala Cinema, Tottenham St. It was besieged by Spandau fans. Suddenly, every record company in Britain was interested.

The fact that most of the band lacked musical ability in any shape or form was irrelevant. Somehow, they *looked* right. Cleverly steered in a profitable direction by Dagger, it was quite obvious from the start that the band's aspirations were commercial rather than artistic. The music they made was styled to reflect the club-scene tastes of the day. Easily-pleased disc jockeys, excited by things different, eagerly hailed Spandau's first

offering **To Cut A Long Story Short** as the best thing since anything spliced.

It looked like Spandau had it made. Few people even noticed that the band had drifted into electro-pop because it is the easiest music for non-musicians to play.

Chrysalis Records eventually won the

rat-race which preceded the band's signing, but still the ever-protective Steve Dagger refused to give anything away. He suddenly found himself having to make the transition from below-the-line manager to tough, mainstream musicbiz boss man, with a penchant for turning music into records and a flourishing underground scene, into a multi-million dollar profit-making concern. With the help of a very good solicitor, instrumental during the Sex Pistols trials, he learned about good and bad deals and fair and unfair contracts. He was as determined as his band not to be ripped of.

> "Working-class kids want to enjoy themselves and look good and be important. That's the kind of lifestyle we grew up with."
>
> **Gary Kemp**

"Take music publishing", he points out. "Nobody wants to tell you what it is, but everybody wants to own it. We've since discovered that it's easy to lose thousands of pounds through the publishing of songs. That's why ours is dealt with solely through our own company, Reformation."

So out went the ugly and in came the glam. The elaborately dolled-up Spandau Ballet put all their money into a dance record and captured the imagination of the industry. Those were risky times indeed — but their timing was perfect. Their first single and first album — **Journeys To Glory**, released a year later in 1981 — made the top five. Possibly a little monotonous, even allowing for their inexperience at that stage, the album nevertheless went gold. Their second,

Diamond, was a definite improvement, but it was not until the release of **True** in 1983, which spawned the band's first Number One hit of the same name, that Spandau Ballet really came into their own. They could now call themselves real musicians. They had learned their trade.

Late in 1983, the ever-verbose Kemp Senior was claiming that Spandau were all set to spearhead a new revolution — the great British Invasion of the American market.

"This country led the world in rock and pop in the sixties", he repeated in a series of interviews at the time. "We lost it in the seventies, when all those angry young men became rather bourgeois and content, but now we have it back, and it's up to us to make the most of it. That's what we need to be selling. It's not just the music, as far as young bands are concerned. It's what they have to say and the way they look. We're not ashamed of that, because we think we do it pretty well. Be innovative. Give it to 'em en bloc."

Duran Duran, however, beat them to it. The band who had leapt so quickly onto the New Romantic bandwagon and copied Spandau's styles with such panache — they, too, grew out of it before it was too late — were already conquering America with a series of spectacular promotional videos, courtesy of MTV, the 24-hour music channel. Spandau Ballet reluctantly took a back seat. Their own videos, although reasonably exotic in their own way, never really measured up to the creativity achieved in the Duran version. Nevertheless, they eventually 'broke' America with one excellent single **True.** Which probably proves that a good song will make it anywhere . . .or that all you need to make it is one good song.

In November 1983, the band undertook a well-received 12-date tour of the States following a mammoth assault on Britain and Europe, during which time they again shocked the industry by staging concerts at such prestigious venues as London's Royal Albert Hall, Royal Festival Hall and Sadler's Wells Theatre. They were never a band to do things by halves. Thus, success now seems assured.

1984 — another album due. This time round they shunned the sun-scorched delights of Compass Point Studios in Nassau, the Bahamas, where they recorded the legendary **True,** in favour of more austere surroundings. In the spring, the band disappeared to Musikland Studios in Munich with ever-faithful producers Tony Swain and Steve Jolley. The result was **Parade,** released in June, which boasts the excellent **Only When You Leave** and **Highly Strung.** Plenty of fans were expecting to be disappointed; how do you improve on a *pièce de résistance* like **True**? They appear to have managed it — with the help of a eager and loyal following.

On, then, to pastures new . . .to Hong Kong and Japan, back to the United States and down under to Australia; ain't no stopping us now. The image has altered drastically since their New Romantic days. From casual to ultra-smart to blatantly butch, the look is currently black and white, leather teamed with sportswear, coolly reminiscent of Wham! Their new-found wealth has furnished near-luxurious lifestyles far-removed from their council-estate days, when they ate what they were given and liked it, and made do with last year's shoes.

Sophisticated socialites with expensive tastes in suits and steering wheels, they are now home-owners to boot. Tony Hadley, the only married member of the band, and his wife Leonie, are the proud parents of a son, Thomas William, born in February 1984. Steve, John, Gary and Martin remain footloose and carefree for now, their names often appearing on the guest lists of film premières and exclusive parties. They are quite partial to a night on the tiles.

So what's new? How long before the bubble bursts? Will they ride on the crest of the musical wave for years to come, or sink without a trace in true fallen-idol tradition? Who knows? Not even Gary Kemp could answer that. One of the most prolific songwriters of the decade, he himself is unlikely to starve. Hadley, meanwhile, has always seen himself as the next Frank Sinatra. With determination and a little careful preservation of his voice, he may well make it. As for Spandau Ballet, they'll no doubt enjoy their success while they can.

Why worry about tomorrow when you can live for today?

SPANDAU BALLET

STYLE COUNCIL

● Paul Weller and Mick Talbot

Hardly anybody could have been surprised when Paul Weller broke up The Jam in December 1982. While others would have milked the astonishing success of the Woking based trio until the cream had curdled and the content had turned rancid, Weller always seemed to have far nobler aspirations for music.

It was Weller who was able to extract the essence of the punk/New Wave ideal and concoct one of Britain's most exciting bands of the past decade. He realised that the cultural revolution of 1976, led by the Sex Pistols, was supposed to lead to a more individual and substantial expres-

sion of music. The energy, power and purity of the classic rockers of the fifties and sixties was to be harnessed and then splintered into a torrent of absorbing tangents. It certainly didn't mean everybody aping The Ramones and singing from the same script.

As a three-piece, The Jam — Weller (guitar), Bruce Foxton (bass) and Rick Buckler (drums) — made their London debut at the 100 Club, the home of punk, in the summer of 1976. They were decked out in clothes reverentially modelled on the sixties' mod look and played speedy, but intelligent, rock numbers, that

revealed a debt to the early work of The Who's Pete Townshend.

In the flurry of record company activity over the next few months due to the punk boom, The Jam were signed by Polydor in February 1977. Their debut single, **In The City,** got to Number 40 in May, while the album of the same name earmarked Weller as a writer of some finesse.

After a shaky start (a patchy second album **This Is The Modern World),** the band released **All Mod Cons,** their third album, which confirmed that The Jam were going to be a major force over the next few years. The single, **Down In The**

Tube Station At Midnight, released at the same time in late 1978, was the start of a glorious chart run in which all their singles made the top 20. In fact *all* their singles made the British top 40.

The album **Setting Sons** unleashed the full power of Weller's compositions. It was a deft and searing examination of the English condition. Here the savage attack of the musicianship was harnessed to some of the most cutting lyrics Weller has ever written. The album reached Number One late in 1979, while

STYLE
COUNCIL

always be remembered for their classic line, *"A man ain't a man with a ticket in his hand"* on **You Need Wheels** (Number 40, August 1979). He'd also played with Dexy's Midnight Runners and their off-shoot The Bureau.

Speak Like A Child reached Number Four in March 1982. It was a mellower Weller after the taut abrasiveness of The Jam. This was a jaunty love song which bounced with the joy of Spring. It showed that the talent of Weller wasn't tied to the politics of anger and concern.

the single **Eton Rifles** made Number Three.

The Jam were at their peak. The next single, **Going Underground,** went straight into the chart at Number One in March 1980 – the first single to do so for seven years. Just to prove it wasn't a fluke, the next single, **Start,** did the same in August the same year. All their singles to that date were simultaneously re-released in April and each one charted in the top 100.

Their work fused brooding, flickering sounds and images of street violence to desperate escapism. In the era of Thatcher's Britain it was no wonder they struck such a resonant chord with a huge core of youth. The Jam had a passionate following that virtually outnumbered the mega stadium fillers. But more importantly, The Jam had created an environment where youth was celebrated, idealism was the highest spiritual value and commitment to your individual

principles was the hard currency.

Despite the success of subsequent albums; **Sound Affects** (1980) and **The Gift** (1982), and singles; **Funeral Pyre** (Number Four, June 1981), **Absolute Beginners** (Number Four, October 1981), **Town Called Malice/Precious** (Number One, February 1982), **Just Who Is The Five O'Clock Hero** (Number Eight, July 1982) and **The Bitterest Pill (I Ever Had To Swallow)** (Number Two, September 1982), things were not right.

There was a feeling that Weller was outgrowing the limitations of a three-piece. The addition of a keyboardist and horn men for their later tours and singles showed Weller's discontent. His songs were getting more introspective and demanded finer shading and texture than a three-piece could provide.

The group's demise was announced in autumn 1982. After an emotional farewell tour, a live album, **Dig The New Breed,** and a single, **Beat Surrender,** which entered the charts at Number One in December, it was all over.

The public didn't have long to wait. Paul Weller (born May 25, 1958) quickly released the first single of The Style Council called **Speak Like A Child.**

The Style Council consisted of himself and Mick Talbot, a keyboardist who had been involved with The Jam since the **Setting Sons** album and appeared on many tours with them.

Talbot (born September 11, 1958 in London) had already had chart success with one of the many 'mod' bands of 1979's revival. The Merton Parkas will

Their second single, **Money-Go-Round,** was an orgy of ideological correctness, but showed that Weller's weakness for meaning and substance had blinded him to what was actually a good record. This dreary and wooden anti-capitalist rap over a mannered funk backing was dreadful. It reached Number 11 in May 1983.

The Style Council **A Paris** EP contained the delirious **Long Hot Summer** and totally captured the glorious summer of 1983. It became a top five hit in June.

His subsequent singles: **Solid Bond In Your Heart** (Number 11, November 1983), **My Ever Changing Moods** (Number Five, February 1984), and **You're The Best Thing** (Number Five, May 1984), and album **Café Bleu,** a top 10 hit in March 1984, have shown Weller at his best.

Though the anger has subsided, the tension and raw talent are still there. While he has refined his sound from the raucous cacophony of **In The City** to the delicate subtlety of **My Ever Changing Moods** (also his first American chart hit in June 1984), he has shown a depth of musical touch that shows he'll be the one to put your money on for the rest of the eighties.

His own label, Respond, has only amassed two hits from Tracie – a girl discovered from an ad in music paper *Smash Hits* – **The House That Jack Built** and **Give Me Some Emotion** in 1983. While that from anybody else would be counted a success, from Weller, you only expect the best.

THOMPSON TWINS

Nature has got nothing on the Thompson Twins when it comes to staggering transformations. Think the chrysalis into butterfly trick is pretty neat? Think a chameleon's skin is one of the most impressive bits of sleight of hand going? Well, I bet even wise old Mother Nature must have stared, open mouthed, at the re-emergence of the Thompson Twins.

From a dishevelled cult outfit, they've turned into one of pop's slickest operators and have become, by mid 1984 one of Britain's top 10 pop money spinners.

The Thompson Twins came into being in 1977. Tom Bailey (vocals, keyboards and percussion), Pete Dodd and John Roog (guitar, vocals and percussion), all friends living in Chesterfield, decided to form a band simply because they enjoyed playing music together.

After gigs in various northern cities, they moved to London and immediately incorporated drummer Chris Bell.

By 1981 the band had expanded to include Joe Leeway (percussion and vocals), Alannah Currie (percussion and sax), and Matthew Seligman (bass).

Their musical direction began to evolve from fast, poppy three minute songs to a more experimental rhythmic sound. They were a band without dogtags, moving in random motion and sniffing puppy-like up each musical lamppost they came across. They spliced folk-rock with funk and a precisely juggled sense of chaos.

The band became famous for hauling the audience on stage to help them smash out an insistent percussive pulse. The result was usually hordes of fans crowding the musicians off the stage in an orgy of drumming.

They were a cult band. They had a tight circle of fans. They were championed by a few journalists who shared their political ideals. And ..., even better for cult status, they didn't sell records.

They were a sprawling seven-piece band of ragamuffin gypsies - hungry for

● Tom Bailey, Alannah Currie and Joe Leeway

something, but not knowing what. They were the ultimate rebels without a cause.

"We were an angry band," says Alannah Currie. "We were angry with the world in general — the deceit and the lies. People grow up with ideals of how things should be and as you grow you open your eyes and get extremely angry. We just continued it."

"At the time," continues Tom Bailey, "there were bands like Joy Division, who were so miserable it made us seem like a bag of fun by comparison. It was a question of climate."

In the studio, songs which had been written with performance in mind proved to be self-indulgent in the cold light of day on vinyl. Their first album, **A Product Of ...,** couldn't surmount this problem on release in June 1981.

Their first singles suffered in the same way. It was only when top producer Steve Lillywhite took an interest in the band late in 1981, that they identified their problem. Lillywhite produced their second album, **Set,** released in February 1982.

While in the studio Tom Bailey wrote **In The Name Of Love,** his first song written primarily for studio and dancefloor. It was intended as an album filler. The single reached Number 79 in the British charts in March 1982.

The single was released in America in April and sailed to the top of the Billboard American disco charts, staying at Number One for five weeks. It also climbed high into the R&B/soul charts. It generated a massive amount of interest in the band and established them as a new musical act capable of penetrating the US market.

The record business had been in a slump since 1978. In America the industry had been trapped in a vicious circle: safe acts leading to dulled audiences, leading to stagnant sales, leading to no-risk A&R policies, leading to more safe acts.

The pattern was broken by two things. First, radio programmers began to realise that their traditional youth market (10-24-year-olds), who still account for 50 per cent of their pop market, was getting bored with the superstar formula. They discovered something that the BBC's Radio One has always known — that good pop radio needs good new sounds. So Britain's new pop successes were the obvious source material for the new US music revival.

But far more importantly, pop radio was forced into its new stance by the advent of MTV – a pop music cable station.

MTV started broadcasting a 24-hour music service in August 1981 and it was quick to provide the hungry market with something fresher than the usual format. The new medium only satisfied their customers out of necessity. When it

began, the only good source of video clips were British performers — video was already an established form of pop promotion in the UK.

The immediate success of Human League and Soft Cell awakened the slumbering giant of the US music industry to the new selling medium. The service works as continuous advertising, since record companies provide their clips for free.

The single returned to its original importance. It was not just a promotional trailer for routine new LPs from the old guard. It was now the ear-grabbing way of getting people to listen to new acts.

What the American market found irresistible was that the British could offer a certain kind of professionalism, musicianship and a strong marketing sense — precisely the sort of things that were thought to be missing from the British rock scene since the punk eruption.

Ironically, prior to news of their American success, The Thompson Twins shed four of their line-up and became triplets. They told everybody they'd gone to Egypt, to create a sense of anticipation about their hibernation, while they worked on a new formula for the Twins in a Norfolk country cottage. In the time honoured rock'n'roll fashion, they 'got it together in the country'.

Much impressed by producer Alex Sadkin's work, the band decided to use his services and left for the Bahamas' Compass Point studios in Nassau to work on their new crop of songs.

They returned with a new image and a sound that was simplicity itself — dribbled synthesiser lines, bouncing percussion and mannered voices.

The triplets were Tom Bailey, Alannah Currie and Joe Leeway.

Bailey was born in Halifax on January 18, 1954. He came from a medical background, with all his family in the profession. He soon became the black sheep of the brood by refusing to follow the planned career. He was also force-fed the piano and the classics, which led his family to thinking he'd become a classical pianist.

He rejected all his family's advice and travelled the world. He was shot at in the Khyber Pass and nearly died after an illness in India.

"As a youngster," he said, "I got taken to Europe a lot, probably before I was old enough to appreciate it, but it became an addiction — being in different places and seeing different cultures. A lot of that was transferred into the aims of the Thompson Twins. We want to be totally international. We're not so naive as to think we can break down barriers, but we can certainly jump over them."

Joe Leeway was born in London's Islington on November 14, 1949. He was born with an Irish mother and a Nigerian father, but was fostered to an English family in Dartford, Kent, from the age of two. He claims he was the only black guy in Dartford and never spoke to another one till he was about 21.

With his father a sailor, his mother and his two sets of foster parents dead, Joe has no family attachments.

He went to college and took English and Drama, then he began teaching English, which was how he met Tom Bailey. He joined a theatre company in Cardiff after failing to establish his own company. Then he went to London's Young Vic theatre for a year, but couldn't land an acting job afterwards. He joined the Thompson Twins as a roadie at Tom Bailey's invitation, but was soon promoted to conga player and full band member.

Alannah Currie was born in New Zealand on September 20, 1957. She was attracted to England after reading about the exploits of Johnny Rotten and the whole punk boom of the late seventies.

"It was the bright lights," she says. "Anyone from an isolated place wants to come to where the action is and you can't get any more isolated than Auckland, New Zealand. We're virtually on the South Pole — you can almost wave to the polar bears from there."

T H E
T H O M P S O N
T W I N S

THO

THE THOMPSON TWINS

A self-confessed non-musician, she nevertheless felt suitably inspired by what she saw and took up 'playing' the saxophone, which she honked formlessly in an all-girl band with an unmentionable name, and then with the Thompson Twins.

"I'd usually come on for the last few numbers," she explains, *"just to add a bit of madness."*

While most bands wouldn't bemoan the loss of their least musically-inclined member, it was Alannah's decision to quit the original Thompsons — initially to pursue goals of her own — that prompted the split and laid the foundations of the Thompsons as they are today.

"After we'd recorded **In The Name Of Love,** *we were so worried that it didn't fit into what the Thompsons were supposed to be about, we seriously considered releasing it under another name — The Bermuda Triangle. Tom, Joe and I had this idea for a kind of Tom Tom Club, an umbrella for all different projects which were outside the scope of the band,"* she recalls.

The Thompson Twins returned from Compass Point as slick business executives. They were a production and marketing company and they were good.

The bohemian sprawl that was the Thompson Twins a few months before, had become a flash corporate machine that was geared up to make the world dance.

They divided their tasks – Tom managed the music, Alannah the visual imagery and Joe the stage production. They took control over every aspect of their output from videos to merchandising.

The name Thompson Twins was derived from Hergé's *Tin Tin* cartoon books. They were a pair of bumbling English detectives, dressed stereotypically in city gent suit and bowlers. The new Thompson Twins took their cartoon origins a stage further – they became cartoons themselves.

They based themselves on the Kelloggs' Snap, Crackle and Pop characters on packets of Rice Krispies. They became a colourful fun package that was perfectly

"After we'd recorded In The Name Of Love, we were so worried that it didn't fit into what the Thompsons were supposed to be about, we seriously considered releasing it under another name — The Bermuda Triangle."

in tune with the new pop of the time.

There was Tom with his pin up poster good looks and flame coloured hair which had a pony tail snaking down his back. There was Joe, dreadlocked and black. And then there was Alannah. Her cascade of blonde hair poking out the front of a giant brimmed French gendarme's cap became the symbol of the Thompson Twins.

They were dressed in the style of all cartoon ragamuffins. It was a perfect formula.

"Cartoons are universal," says Joe. *"Everybody understands them and it's an easy way to put ideas across."*

The first single from the Alex Sadkin sessions was **Lies** from October 1982. It reached Number 67 in Britain, but followed its predecessor into the American charts, where it hit the top slot in the disco charts.

The British breakthrough came with **Love On Your Side** in January 1983. It cracked the top 10 and they haven't looked back since. Their third album, their first as the new dynamic face of pop, called **Quick Step And Side Kick,**

reached Number Two in the charts in February 1983.

The tango style **We Are Detective** (Number Eight in May 1983) showed that they could successfully negotiate non-dance tunes and have hits.

Watching was a relative failure, reaching only 33 in the British singles chart in July 1983, but this was only a brief lull.

Hold Me Now became one of the big Christmas hits of 1983 and the record that cracked the US market wide open for them. The single reached Number Four in Britain and was a top five record in America. The album **Into The Gap** catapulted the Thompson Twins into the list of Britain's top 10 pop earners. It entered the British charts at Number One on its first week of release in February 1984. The single **Doctor Doctor** reached Number Three in the same month while **You Take Me Up** went one place better in April 1984.

"We planned it," says Alannah. *"I thought we were being overambitious — but it's all going according to plan — and we've only just started."*

MINS

U2

In December 1979, the nine people who watched a young Dublin quartet called U2 going through their paces in the dank cellar of London's Hope and Anchor pub, had no idea that, three and a half years later, the same outfit would play to 25,000 people at Dublin's Phoenix Park. In the time between, several musical revolutions would come and go, but U2's supercharged, aerodynamic reworking of rock could hardly fail.

Apparently it was drummer Larry Mullen who'd had the original idea of forming the band, back in 1977. Larry, bassist Adam Clayton, singer Paul "Bono Vox" Hewson and guitarist Dave "The Edge" Evans all met at Dublin's Mount Temple school, Ireland's first 'progressive comprehensive', though Clayton had earlier done time at boarding school. In the event, the foursome emerged from Mount Temple mercifully free from religious sectarianism, something they view in retrospect as an unmixed blessing.

Aided by manager Paul McGuinness, who already had a successful career as a director of commericals, U2 swiftly began to build a keen local following, and released an EP called **U23** on CBS Ireland. But it wasn't until they signed to Island Records and released the memorable **11 O'Clock Tick Tock** single that ears began to prick up further afield. **11 O'Clock** was produced by Martin Hannett, who'd worked with U2's heroes Joy Division, and it gave an early glimpse of the extraordinary acrobatics of which Edge's guitar was capable.

By autumn 1980, U2 had toured Britain and were installed in Dublin's Windmill Lane studios with producer Steve Lillywhite. The results, an album called **Boy,** appeared in October, and it caused a *frisson* of excitement in reviewers and public alike. Even the sleeve was striking, showing a young boy gazing wide-eyed into the world with an uncanny, knowing innocence. The music inside was full of light and space, both graceful and

powerful. From Edge's scalding introduction to **I Will Follow**, it was obvious that this band was fuelled on a different kind of tension, and was willing to learn, but not to capitulate.

From the start, U2 had made it clear that they didn't intend to be a mere 'rock group' like all the other ones. Certain spiritual inclinations could be discerned within the lucid structures of their music, and would become more explicit with subsequent releases. Bono, galvanic singer and non-stop spokesman for the group, explained: *"I'm not anti-drink . . . all of us drink occasionally. But I don't think we're involved in what I call rock'n'roll masturbation, which is that you're in a band, you get wrecked with other bands, and it gets in the papers and everybody laughs, ho ho ho."*

A year after **Boy,** they released a second long-player called **October.** By now, they'd tackled a three-month American tour and scored a first chart single in

Fire. New songs with titles like **Gloria** and **Rejoice** now began to earn Bono a few brickbats for his evangelical tendencies and religious inclinations, while others insisted that the new album was merely an inferior retread of its predecessor. This didn't prevent it from entering

the British chart at 11.

Certainly, Steve Lillywhite's production this time around was harder, louder, less impressionistic, but there were plenty of moments of high drama, while **Tomorrow** was positively ominous. U2 were

becoming less ethereal, but there was no loss of power.

After **October** it was back to the USA, where business was booming – not least because of an enthusiastic endorsement from Bruce Springsteen, the New Jersey Messiah. Meanwhile, American crowds were learning to love the almost Who-like presence which U2 were capable of generating on a good night. *"The guitar, bass and drum set-up is good for giving people a good slap in the face,"* Bono would say succinctly of the band's very basic instrumental line-up.

U2 spent the bulk of 1982 either in the States or playing vast European festivals (though they also played at Gateshead with The Police). From a British perspective, it looked as though the group were quite content to plough the well-worn rock furrow, simplifying their music to please zombie-like stadium crowds and conveniently forgetting their early idealism. Apocryphal–sounding stories abounded of their religious zeal even while on tour, with the less fanatical Adam Clayton forced to wait until the others had gone to sleep before getting wrecked with the road-crew. Some of their supporters were becoming sceptical.

They came back with a bang in January 1983, with a new single and an album called **War. New Year's Day** rapidly breached the top ten singles chart, and was inspired by Polish Solidarity leader Lech Walesa. The album (produced by Lillywhite once more) instantly went to the very top of the album charts in

Britain, and later made a beeline for the American top ten.

War opened with Larry's armour-piercing drum intro to **Sunday Bloody Sunday,** Bono's most explicit-ever shot at a song about Northern Ireland. Not long after the album's release, U2 played the song in Belfast. *"I did a five-minute rap on stage explaining the song, and said, 'if you don't like it, say so, and we'll never sing it again,'"* Bono recalled. He needn't have worried – three people walked out,

while the rest roared their support. Whether or not you approve of U2 and their breast-beating performances, it has to be admitted that few groups ever took it *this* close to the bone.

At the Phoenix Park festival in August 1983, a momentous occasion which also featured Big Country, Eurythmics and Simple Minds, some observers felt dissatisfied with U2's climactic set. The sound verged on crass heavy metal, while Bono's white flag and determination to climb the PA had by now become so familiar from other shows and TV broadcasts, that it seemed U2 might be heading for a lot of Sunday Nights at the London Palladium.

The release in November of the live mini-LP **Under A Blood Red Sky** was consequently something of a relief for the group's devotees. It comprised the highlights of a typical U2 live set, and caught the band in peculiarly incandescent form. **11 O'Clock Tick Tock** far outstripped the original recording, while the closing **40** seemed to float out over the heads of a crowd of thousands like a benediction.

Meanwhile, U2 were rumoured to be having trouble writing material for a new studio album, while the news that the disc would be produced by ambient egg-head Brian Eno left many pundits suppressing a chortle. And could it really be true that Bono planned to leave the group to pursue a career in Irish politics?

With the next LP scheduled for the autumn, U2 are currently under wraps. Whatever happens, they'll be remembered for some rare moments of fire and atmosphere, though not even their most devout disciples could accuse them of expanding the limited vocabulary of rock.

In the era of MTV and micro-electronics, U2 reminded thousands of fans of what used to make rock tick. As Bono had said early in the group's career: *"We were inspired by New Yorkers like Patti Smith and Television, rather than the Sex Pistols. But we did have this spark, because the music takes second place to the emotion, and that's how it is today."*

UB40

When UB40 first got together in the summer of 1978, their music – if you can call it that – had a distinct Brum accent. Six years on the accent's still there, but it's acquired inflections and nuances that the Third World would be proud of.

All eight members are British born, four of them white. They were all brought up in the multi-cultural, working class communities of south central Birmingham, where reggae music was as much part of their daily diet as chicken vindaloo.

The original line-up didn't include Mickey or Astro, but it did include two musicians – Jimmy Lynn, who played keyboards, and a Nigerian percussionist known as Yomi. They were not to remain with the band for long, quickly becoming disenchanted with the total ineptitude.

Fortunately the desire to play was so great that the remainder learned their various instruments in a matter of weeks. They practised daily in the cellar below the house where bass player Earl Falconer, and would-be saxophonist Brian Travers, lived at the time.

Mickey Virtue joined in January 1979, and together they played their first gig on February 9th at a local pub called the Hare and Hounds in Kings Heath. They

can't have been too bad, because local bookings started pouring in. The band rapidly outgrew the Midlands pub circuit, and began appearing around the country, especially in London.

It was during this period that Astro completed the line-up which has remained ever since. It was still early days and they weren't technically great, but they more than made up for it with their enthusiasm, dedication and freshness – something that is still with them today, and of course they are now technically proficient as well.

They recorded a demo tape at the same studio where they were to later record **Signing Off** and their first single **King/Food For Thought,** and sent it to a local commercial radio station. The jocks there loved it and the BBC's John Peel was equally impressed. He arranged a session which was then broadcast on his Radio One programme in January 1980.

Chrissie Hynde probably carried more weight than John (metaphorically speaking, of course), and when she saw them play at Dingwall's and again at the Rock Garden, she asked them to support the Pretenders on their British tour.

It was during that tour that the first single was released, the group having

signed during December '79 to Graduate Records, a small independent company in nearby Dudley. It was an almost overnight success, rising rapidly to Number Four in the national chart, and was the first single ever to reach the top ten without the backing of a major record company. There were two more hit singles on Graduate as well as the debut album, **Signing Off,** which stayed in the chart for over a year. The contract with Graduate expired in December 1980 and the band formed their own record company, DEP International. DEP's first two album releases, **Present Arms** and **Present Arms In DUB** joined **Signing Off** in the chart, towards the end of that year.

James Brown, the singing drummer, no longer had to talk himself into cushy office jobs (he had a knack of charming the personnel officer, ending up in easy jobs that he was totally unqualified for), as he was now earning enough to pay the rent and have the odd night out. Not that his nights out cost much, he usually spent them with friends debating social and political matters: he has been described as a 'talkative anarchist'. Born on November 20, 1957, he went to Marlborough Road Primary School and Moseley Road School Of Art, where he became friends with Ali, Earl and Brian.

Most groups have a token art school member, but not four! And all at the same school. It was obviously a good breeding ground for music, but the track record for producing painters – if UB40 are anything to go by – is pathetic. James ended up in an office, Earl was a plasterer, Brian an electrician and Ali couldn't even get a job as a plasterer.

Ali Campbell spent those three unemployed years absorbing the music he loved. His evocative singing is an integral part of UB40, but he would much rather play instrumental dub reggae; in spite of being a rhythm guitarist par excellence, he's most interested in drums and bass. He was born on February 15, 1959 and went to St. Luke's Junior School prior to the art school.

You could say Brian Travers' formal training paid off slightly, as he is largely responsible for the band's videos and the

UB40

visual side of their work. Born on February 7, 1959, he went to Cape Hill and Lakey Lane Primary Schools and then joined the others at art school.

Completing the art school quartet is Earl Falconer, who was born on January 23, 1959. He attended St. Benedict's Junior School, as did his brother Ray, who is the band's excellent sound engineer.

Robin Campbell plays guitar and sings. He didn't when he attended St. Paul's Primary School or George Dixon's Grammar School, but he loathed school so much there wasn't a lot to sing about. He was born on Christmas Day in 1954. UB40's the longest job he's ever had; before joining the band he had at least 30.

Norman Lamont Hassan was born on January 26, 1957, and went to school at Tindall Street and Queensbridge Road. Before taking up percussion and the trombone, he was a carpet layer. He

doesn't socialise with the band as much now because he's a devoted family man.

Michael Virtue was born on January 19, 1957, and attended Clifton Road Primary School and Golden Hillock Comprehensive. He was working in an office when he joined UB40. Although reggae is his main source of inspiration, he is influenced by jazz and jazz-funk.

Astro toasts (talks over) and plays trumpet. He is also the show's self-appointed MC. He met the band at one of the Moseley pub shows and insisted on joining them there and then. Born June 24, 1957, he went to Greet and Golden Hillock Schools.

The band's third album **Present Arms** was the first dub album to enter the national pop charts, and the first to be stocked by chain stores. During 1981 the band toured the USA, Britain, Europe (twice), Australia and New Zealand. In 1982 they toured Zimbabwe — an

interesting, if harrowing, experience. During 1983 they kept on trekking, this time to Japan and two return trips to North America (which included several dates with the Police).

The fourth album **UB44,** featured the first ever hologram sleeve — a limited edition released only in the UK.

In 1983, **Labour Of Love** was released and the first single taken from it, **Red, Red Wine** went to Number One. **Labour Of Love** is a selection of other people's songs, a project that had been discussed since their formation: their own interpretation of just a few of the reggae hits, which had inspired their love of the music, at the turn of the seventies.

Apart from being one of Britain's most consistently impressive 'live' acts, they have also earned respect on the reggae scene itself, for not only have they absorbed the music, they also passionately endorse its message.

UB40

Are Wham! too big for their boots? Of course they are! What's more they'll be the first to admit it. They both know that those expensive clothes and suntanned smiles are just a distraction. Wham! don't want to change the world . . . far from it. They just want to take your mind off the pressures of everyday life.

"What are people supposed to do with their lives apart from enjoy them? We just play for those who are prepared to feel happy . . . I don't want people to say that our music is incredibly innovative, I just want them to enjoy it."

George Michael and Andrew Ridgeley, two soul boys, not to mention soul mates, steered a passage out of the dole queue and into the charts back in 1982. But let's pick up the story some seven years earlier.

The two met when George became a new boy at Bushey Heath Comprehensive in Hertfordshire. A time Andrew well remembers: "We were in the schoolyard playing a game called 'king of the wall' and this new kid called George pushed me off. You could say that's where our friendship began!"

After leaving school, the two blazed a trail through their local nightclubs, where they developed a keen interest in imported dance music. Both admit that they spent an unhealthy amount of time chasing the night life, and although the pair didn't realise it at the time, this period was to be the key to their success. For under the glare of the fluorescent lights, George and Andrew evolved a style that a few years later became the perfect antidote to the doom and gloom of the post punk era. People thought hard times were here to stay, but Wham! had other ideas.

However, that's not to say that George and Andrew have always been the supremely confident wheeler-dealers behind those squeaky-clean dancefloor hits. There were times during Wham!'s formative years of the late seventies when both despaired of ever leaving the unemployment jungle.

There was one particular occasion when a despondent Andrew sat in George's kitchen, ready to give up the idea of getting Wham! off the ground. It was a course of action that would have pleased their parents no end, as they wanted their boys to move into respectable professions like law and accountancy.

George knew though that the duo were too far down the road to turn back. He reasoned with his partner that it was too easy to throw away the dreams and ambitions which had been years in the making.

Like the time when they formed a ska band called the Executive which dealt in those primitive R'n'B rhythms so popular in the late seventies. And their first gig!

WHAM!

The local scout hut hasn't been the same since the Executive shattered its foundations with a set that nearly deafened their friends.

Their apprenticeship spent treading the club boards and pouring over the import racks at record shops hadn't been for nothing, had it?

The partners in crime talked well into the night, and after their highly charged exchange, George and Andrew emerged stronger than ever. And so they set about pooling their meagre resources to record a song they'd just written called **Wham Rap.**

So with just £20 to their name, Wham! bought enough studio time to record a demo. George sang lead vocal and played bass, while Andrew concentrated on guitar and the drum machine. Within a short time they'd created that soft funk style people now take for granted. That was January 1982.

It wasn't long before that tape fell in to the lap of a young man called Mark Dean. Dean typified a new breed of young record company executive. He hadn't long turned 20 and was already running his own label, Innervision.

Dean knew that the time was right for a change of direction in modern music. So times were tough in a country plagued by unemployment, but people didn't have to be reminded of it the whole time. Wham!'s no-nonsense approach couldn't have been better timed. Dean snapped them up.

Wham Rap was released as their debut single, and it soon became a great favourite in the clubs, but at the BBC it was a different story. The corporation didn't see the joke in lyrics that extolled the virtues of life on the dole.

So **Wham Rap**'s sales drive lost impetus, but waves had been made, and their next single, **Young Guns,** was the clincher. **Young Guns** was a sideswipe at young couples who'd settled for marriage as an easy alternative. George and Andrew poured scorn on those that lacked the drive and ambition to live life out on the edge, where your only responsibilities are to yourself.

"I wrote the song after watching a programme on TV, which was about how a lot of people were getting married younger and younger. The bit that hit me was when they interviewed two really young guys in a pub, who explained that the reason they were getting married was because all their mates had done the same thing, and they wouldn't have anyone to go out drinking with."

Needless to say, a sizeable portion of Wham!'s generation heeded their advice and **Young Guns** peaked at Number Three in the charts in December 1982.

Another selling point had been the impressive choreography that was an integral part of Wham!'s live shows and TV appearances, and this is where the duo's backing singers Shirlie Holliman and Dee C. Lee came into their own. Like George and Andrew, the girls had spent

"We were in the schoolyard playing a game called 'king of the wall' and this new kid called George pushed me off. You could say that's where our friendship began!"

Andrew Ridgeley

WHAM!

> "While I don't regret anything we've done musically, I do regret the image we ended up with for Bad Boys."
>
> George Michael

their later teenage years dancing in clubs, and with the girl's well rehearsed moves acting as the perfect foil to the collective brashness of George and Andrew, the spectacle was complete.

Young Guns was not without its critics, though. Some people felt that the lyric reinforced the stereotype of the devil-may-care boy about town being doted on by an adoring, insecure girlfriend.

"We were trying to treat a serious situation in a lighthearted way," explained George. *"The idea that the woman wants security before the man is very much a natural thing. There are basic differences between the two sexes. For example, it's the woman who gets lumbered with the baby, and needs the security more than the man does. So, to me, the single rang very true."*

After the huge success of **Young Guns,** the time seemed right to re-release **Wham Rap,** and this time nothing could stop it. The BBC had relaxed its policy slightly, and the single sneaked through the net, reaching Number Eight in February 1983.

The Wham! guide to better living was beginning to take root, and a third hit single wasn't long in coming. **Bad Boys** saw George and Andrew acting out different roles, and this time they were the macho motorcycle boys who turned their tricks on the wrong side of the tracks. But it's an image George is none too sure about.

"While I don't regret anything we've *done musically, I do regret the image we ended up with for* **Bad Boys.** *It was written as a humourous song, and was meant to be tongue in cheek, but it didn't come across that way in the video. I hate it!"*

Despite George's criticism, the single still got to Number Two in May 1983. But Wham! sensed the need to slow the pace of their music a little, and so decided to re-work their sound away from rap tinged funk towards a more atmospheric, lush sounding production. **Club Tropicana** was the result, proving to Wham!'s sternest critics that they were capable of engineering different sounding records.

Although **Club Tropicana** became the

duo's fourth hit in July 1983, there was a sizeable section of the music press vehemently opposed to Wham!'s live for today approach, and with the release of their first LP, **Fantastic,** the old criticisms were once again levelled at the twosome. Firstly that title, **Fantastic,** wasn't it rather self-congratulatory? And didn't it set the tone for a collection of songs that were at best smug, and at worst downright conceited?

Well, not in the record buyer's eyes, because **Fantastic** shot up to the top of the album charts in summer of 1983, which meant that in under 12 months, Wham! had sold a total of two and a half million records.

So the former dole boys had become household names, and the reason for that success is due in no small way to the fanatical following the duo have managed to attract. Their live shows sell out within hours, and it's usually great hordes of adoring, teenage girls that snap up the tickets. And their fans are seldom disappointed, as a lot of work goes into their stage productions — things like exotic sets and numerous costume changes all designed to titillate those onlookers.

"Here we are with all these women following us, but you find you don't want to take advantage of it. It's so hard getting past people's image of you."

Still it's no secret that at one time Andrew went around with backing singer Shirlie, and very strong rumours have circulated about a liaison between George and singer Hazel O'Connor. So maybe the boys are just being coy.

Backing singer Shirlie for her part has been dated by Spandau Ballet's Martin

Wham! break-up, George made plans for that first solo single, and settled on veteran producer Jerry Wexler to man the console. It didn't work out. After something like £100,000 was spent on its production, George decided that Wexler's work was too dated — the man's past credits had included people like Wilson Pickett and Aretha Franklin.

George decided to handle the production duties himself, and a totally new

However, it hasn't been all plain sailing. Towards the end of 1983, Wham! fell out with their record company Innervision over the sum due to them from record sales.

A protracted legal battle was fought, during which Innervision released the **Club Fantastic Megamix** single, which the twosome refused to promote. In the end Wham! were forced to settle out of court, and the boys were pretty much back to square one financially. However, they have enlisted the services of notorious music business entrepreneur Simon Napier-Bell as their manager, which should help their cause considerably.

Although plotting a successful pop music career is a full-time business, George and Andrew still have plenty of time for girls, though not steady girlfriends they claim. Andrew is in no doubt as to where Wham!'s appeal lies, *"A lot of people realise they're good looking, and we're the same. George and I aren't vain, just realistic!"*

"It's funny, you know," says George,

Kemp, which really came as no surprise as Wham! and Spandau have been the best of friends for some years.

The other Wham! girl, Dee C. Lee, left the duo in 1983 to concentrate on other singing projects and was replaced by Pepsi, a former session singer.

1984 saw Wham! sort out their legal problems, and the group signed to a new label, Epic. However, the lengthy legal battle with their former label, Innervision, had put untold pressure on George and Andrew, and rumours started to circulate about a possible split.

Speculation heightened when George announced that he was planning a solo single called **Careless Whisper,** although the pair maintained that their working relationship was stronger than ever.

The doubters were soon silenced. Wham! came storming back with their debut release for Epic called **Wake Me Up Before You Go Go,** an infectious slice of Summer pop, which entered the charts at Number Four, reaching the top a week later in June 1984.

Having dispelled the rumours of a

version of **Careless Whisper** was recorded for Summer '84 release.

So Wham! are back on course, celebrating youth and good times, swilling cocktails in exotic locations, posing for centrefold spreads with pouting lips and hinting at social trends without sloganeering.

In fact, George and Andrew are ambivalent when it comes to political solutions. Both have said that they would play in South Africa if they thought it wouldn't harm their careers, yet both voted Labour in the last election.

Neither deny their single-minded quest to be the best group in the world, and nothing, they claim, will get in their way. George cites one reason above all else for their success in the face of adversity: *"Wham! is the result of a close friendship. We've been friends for eight or nine years — and that's in spite of Andrew's bad taste and revolting habits!"*

● Andrew Ridgeley

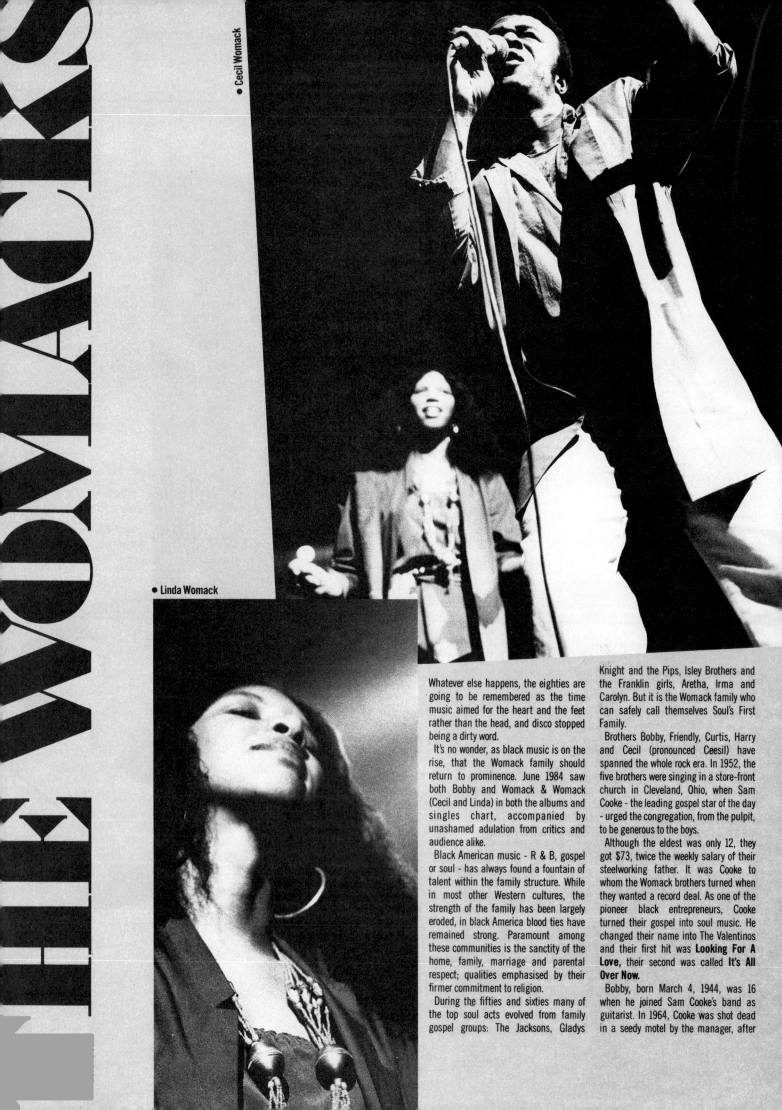

THE WOMACKS

● Cecil Womack

● Linda Womack

Whatever else happens, the eighties are going to be remembered as the time music aimed for the heart and the feet rather than the head, and disco stopped being a dirty word.

It's no wonder, as black music is on the rise, that the Womack family should return to prominence. June 1984 saw both Bobby and Womack & Womack (Cecil and Linda) in both the albums and singles chart, accompanied by unashamed adulation from critics and audience alike.

Black American music - R & B, gospel or soul - has always found a fountain of talent within the family structure. While in most other Western cultures, the strength of the family has been largely eroded, in black America blood ties have remained strong. Paramount among these communities is the sanctity of the home, family, marriage and parental respect; qualities emphasised by their firmer commitment to religion.

During the fifties and sixties many of the top soul acts evolved from family gospel groups: The Jacksons, Gladys Knight and the Pips, Isley Brothers and the Franklin girls, Aretha, Irma and Carolyn. But it is the Womack family who can safely call themselves Soul's First Family.

Brothers Bobby, Friendly, Curtis, Harry and Cecil (pronounced Ceesil) have spanned the whole rock era. In 1952, the five brothers were singing in a store-front church in Cleveland, Ohio, when Sam Cooke - the leading gospel star of the day - urged the congregation, from the pulpit, to be generous to the boys.

Although the eldest was only 12, they got $73, twice the weekly salary of their steelworking father. It was Cooke to whom the Womack brothers turned when they wanted a record deal. As one of the pioneer black entrepreneurs, Cooke turned their gospel into soul music. He changed their name into The Valentinos and their first hit was **Looking For A Love,** their second was called **It's All Over Now.**

Bobby, born March 4, 1944, was 16 when he joined Sam Cooke's band as guitarist. In 1964, Cooke was shot dead in a seedy motel by the manager, after

Cooke allegedly assaulted a call-girl.

Since then both the Womacks and the Cookes have remained close - really close. First Bobby tied the knot with Sam Cooke's widow, Barbara. Cecil married Mary Wells - later to write her name in pop history as the singer of one of Motown's finest pop songs, **My Guy**, in 1964. Both couples divorced.

In 1977, Cecil remarried; his bride was Sam and Barbara Cooke's daughter, Linda. And, in a move that made Dallas look like reality, Curtis Womack married Mary Wells.

After Sam Cooke's death, Bobby Womack found himself playing guitar in Memphis for the legendary Atlantic label. He backed Aretha Franklin, King Curtis, Dusty Springfield and Wilson Pickett.

"At the time I was making $150,000 a year as a sideman and it was in Memphis that I discovered I had a talent for producing.

"Say, we were in there cutting Joe Tex's **Skinny Legs 'N' All,** *I'd come up with the intro. Then it would be, 'hey man, I got another idea', and everybody would be saying 'yeah, yeah'. They paid me triple scale! That was sweet. And Joe Tex said to me, 'Bobby, that guy in there ain't producing, he's using all your ideas'. I knew Wilson Pickett from the gospel world, so I started producing him. I had a bunch of songs I'd written planning to cut myself, but I gave them to him. Stuff like* **634-5789, Midnight Hour** *and* **Midnight Mover."**

But what shot Bobby into the public eye was his old song **It's All Over Now** becoming a worldwide hit - the first for a scruffy bunch of English R & B fans called the Rolling Stones in 1964. It was also their first Number One hit in Britain.

The Valentinos' **Looking For A Love** became the first chart success for the J Geils Band in 1972.

It was Bobby Womack's **Breezin'** that turned jazz guitarist George Benson into an internationally famous star in 1976. The album of the same name became the first jazz album to sell more than a million copies.

To the Rolling Stones' Ron Wood, and Leon Russell, Bobby Womack is a first rate producer and arranger of their music.

To Rod Stewart, Eric Clapton, Herbie Hancock and Santana, Bobby has been a source of writing, producing and performing.

"Whenever I see Rod," says Bobby, *"he tells me, man, you're great, and always mentions my name or Sam Cooke. He says 'these are guys I listen to and they're the ones who deserve the credit'."*

"You know, he once had me come down to a session and sing a song because he wanted to copy the way I sang it. The song was **Do Ya Think I'm Sexy?"**

Bobby Womack signed his first recording contract in 1968. His third album **Communication** gave him his first solo chart success in America with **That's The Way I Feel About Cha** in 1972. The next album, **Understanding** (recorded only days after **Communication**), gave him three hit singles in 1973 with **Woman's Gotta Have It, Sweet Caroline** and **Harry Hippie.** Sadly his recording career has never been as consistent as his considerable talent.

Drug abuse through the seventies bought him a reputation for being volatile and difficult, and his record sales declined.

Following a four year hiatus - brought on by the death of youngest brother Harry, stabbed by a jealous girlfriend in 1978 - he returned with **The Poet.** He was signed to Beverly Glen records, a small independent label — the only one that would have him. The record sold one and a half million copies in 1982.

1984's **Poet II** has not only consolidated Bobby's success but magnified it.

Away from the spotlight, brother Cecil and Linda were quietly building their own careers as songwriters, composing hits for artists like Teddy Pendergrass, Millie Jackson and the O'Jays. The pair deliberately refused to tour or record until their 1983 debut album **Love Wars** - the title track becoming a huge British hit in May 1984.

The success of both Bobby and Womack & Womack are notable because they've run against the electro and dance tide, and come through strongly with the traditional black music values of impassioned singing and well-crafted melodies.

"When we came along singing gospel you needed two good feet and some lungs on you", says Cecil. *"Nowadays people are just chasing commercialism; but if you stay with what you believe long enough, your time will always come around."*

So it is that after 30 years in the business the Womack brood are suddenly overnight successes. But the past is only just behind them. Bobby Womack's new manager is Allen Klein - famed for his association with the Beatles and the Stones, but who started out managing . . .Sam Cooke. Klein is planning a Broadway musical on the life of Cooke, but Bobby Womack prefers a film and has volunteered himself for the title role.

The four remaining Womack brothers have reformed the Valentinos and have recently completed an album in Los Angeles.

Quips Bobby, *"We drift apart sometimes,"* says Bobby, *"but we always end up back together again. The word Womack means family."*

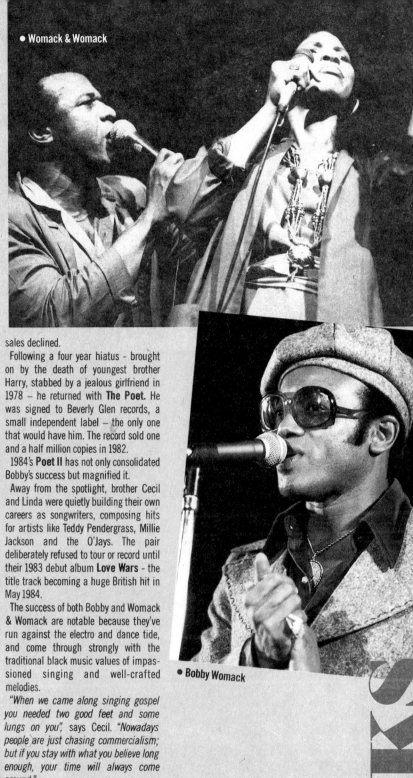

● Womack & Womack

● Bobby Womack

THE WOMACKS

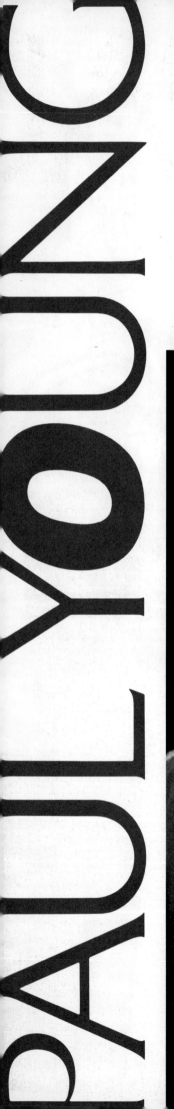

PAUL YOUNG

Open up any pop magazine and there he is! The pearly white teeth, well groomed hair and designer suits are proof positive that Paul Young has hit the big time.

To look at him now, you'd never think that Paul had to struggle to reach the dizzy heights of the pop world, but it's been a long and arduous road to the top.

Born in Luton on January 17, 1956, Paul displayed all the characteristics of your typical Capricorn. As a small boy he was shy and sensitive, although was given to the occasional outburst. Like the time he sang a few songs on the local bus and earned a standing ovation from the other passengers. Paul's father was amazed, his young son was all of two years old!

This early singing experience was put to good use a few years later, when Paul became a choirboy at a nearby church. Paul's father, Tony, well remembers his son's efforts: *"He seemed to enjoy his singing, and he liked weddings best — he could pick up a few bob then!"*

As Paul grew up, he showed flair for the creative subjects at Luton's Ashcroft High School, and hated the science based subjects like physics. Most of all though, he enjoyed his school dinners, along with everyone else's come to that, and so became known as 'Dustbin Hoffman'!

When Paul was 14, his father encouraged him to take piano lessons, and this proved to be a turning point in the young man's life. It wasn't long before the would-be musician switched to bass guitar, then singing, due to a shortage of talented young singers in Luton.

Although Paul's friends were enthusing about hard rock and heavy metal groups around at the time, the nearest Paul came to that was his love

for the blues tainted rock band Free. Vocalist Paul Rodgers was a major source of inspiration, and from here Paul went on to explore some of the greatest names in blues and soul – Otis Redding, Sam Cooke and Joe Tex.

Paul at this stage had already left school with six O levels, and had joined the Vauxhill car plant as an apprentice. Although, both his father and elder brother Mark were already working there, Paul found it difficult to settle.

The fact that he was played for a local group called Streetband didn't help, and so the young singer was faced with a choice. It wasn't a difficult one to make – with his father's backing, Paul joined Streetband full-time, and so began his uncomfortable association with heavy metal.

The group managed to dent the charts back in the Autumn of 1978 with a novelty hit, **Toast.** It was the success of

PA

PAUL
YOUNG

same year. To cap it all, the LP which spawned those three hits, **No Parlez** reached Number One in the LP charts, and sold over a million copies in the process.

Top of Paul's huge list of priorities is to continue looking for the right material to record. He and producer Laurie Latham are for ever sifting through van loads of material. Paul still relies on other composers for his songs, as he sees his role as one of interpretation rather than composition.

Paul would be the first to admit that his success must be due in part to the enviable backing band he's built around him. The Royal Family provide the perfect backdrop of Paul's plaintive voice, and The Fabulous Wealthy Tarts – Kim and Maz to their friends – Paul's celebrated backing singers, round off the sound beautifully.

Away from the spotlight, Paul makes sure he has the time for the important things in life like family and friends. Both sets help to run his ever growing fan club, and his brother, Mark, even has to look after Paul's prized possession – his Datsun 280 Turbo sports car, while the singer's away on tour.

On the romance front, the Luton heart throb has been linked with a number of girls during his career. Names like Tracie, Mari Wilson and Supergirl actress Helen Slater spring to mind, though Paul strenuously denies these associations. In fact it was only a short while ago that he split up with his long time girlfriend, who works for a record promotions company.

When it's time to relax, Paul enjoys an Indian meal washed down by tequila and orange juice. Or if there's an old James Stewart film on TV, he'll quite happily stay at home in his North London flat.

But with such a heavy workload, Paul seldom has much time off, and one engagement that will stick in his mind is when he headlined at The Prince's Trust Rock Gala in June 1984. It was a case of one Royal Family meeting another as Paul and the group played before the Prince and Princess Of Wales in aid of underprivileged children.

Princess Diana is said to be a big fan of Paul's, and let's face it, with connections like those, there's no way the boy can lose!

that single that killed them off as Paul admits: *"We used to get married couples coming to the gigs expecting to see The Barron Knights or something. But when we came on and did a really heavy opening — all guitar solos and that, it didn't take long for them to leave!"*

The heavy metal material was taking it's toll on Paul's voice too, and when he damaged his throat muscles, Paul decided to leave the group. There followed some months of deep depression.

"I couldn't face the car factory again, and was just wondering what to do next, when this offer came to join Q Tips — I jumped at it!"

An eight-piece soul group, dedicated to all the principles that Paul held dear. It sounded heaven sent, and to start with it was.

As you might expect, there was never a dull moment on a Q Tips tour. Paul remembers times when they nailed up the front doors to guest houses after the owners had been unnecessarily rude to them!

The group had signed to Chrysalis Records, but struggle as they might, the company couldn't capture their powerful live sound on vinyl. Despite skirting the charts with a thumping version of Joe

Tex's *S.Y.S.L.J.F.M.*, Q Tips parted company, broke and dispirited.

The news wasn't all bad though. Paul had been offered numerous record deals as a solo artist, and so later in that same year of 1982, he signed on the dotted line with CBS Records.

The singer immediately got to work with producer Laurie Latham, but his first two solo singles **Iron Out The Rough Spots** and **Love of The Common People** flopped chart-wise, and record company executives became deeply worried. It's a time Paul's producer Laurie Latham recalls only too well.

"There was much wringing of hands and talk about changing the team. Then Paul's A and R man got up and suggested Paul's cover version of Marvin Gaye's **Wherever I Lay My Hat** *as a single. We all laughed and told the guy to sing it to us if he felt it was so strong.*

"To his credit he did. So Paul and I went back to the studio, tarted it up and the rest is history."

Indeed it is. **Wherever I Lay My Hat** made the Number One spot for three weeks in August 1983, and this paved the way for **Come Back And Stay** and a re-release of **Love Of The Common People** to make the top five later the

THE ROCK REVIEW

SCENE OF THE

by Pete Johnson

...e have to live for, man. Day and night ..." Errol tells me. Looking at the dour ...scape that surrounds us, it's hard to ...plication of those words. Obsessions ...es of austerity and, as a multitude of ...s, Wham! fans or headbangers will ...ave to put your faith *somewhere*.
...sic is reggae. Not the over-produced, ...ff that from time to time slips under ...ners' net and onto the airwaves, but ...gae. At thrice-weekly, all-night house

...cs

parties the latest Jamaican imports, amplified to wall-shaking volume by his cousin's rentable sound system, provide a soundtrack for their high times. As an outsider peering into the smoke-filled room with its dozens of gently swaying bodies, you quickly realise that it's a serious way to have fun.

Reggae in the mid-eighties stands on the stage but away from the glare of the spotlight. The music which bursts out of a Third World ghetto in the mid-seventies, to the acclaim of rock audiences

● Dennis Brown

● Aswad

● Sugar Minott

bored with the state of pop, has taken a step back to its roots. Major labels, who, encouraged by rave reviews from the hipper end of the pop press, had a decade ago fallen over each other in the rush to sign their very own reggae star, have steadily backed away, and with them they have taken much of the incentive to record. Singers who once bombarded the market with releases now languish in obscurity, releasing the occasional tune that sells in hundreds and is forgotten in a month. In the music business, money sings. People on the breadline can seldom afford to make music for the love of it.

But, it would be wrong to assume that reggae has lost its direction. Although the musical virtuosity and complex harmonies that epitomised so much seventies reggae have given way to a rougher, drum and bass dominated sound, it remains an irresistibly melodious music. The influence of the late Bob Marley, well-publicised by rock group the Police, has left few visible marks on contemporary Jamaican music. In place of the meticulous arrangements and considered Rastafarian lyricism, today's hot disco-mix is likely to feature throwaway lyrics proclaiming the singer's fatal attraction for women and a backing track you already possess ten times over. The process of re-using popular bass-lines (or 'rhythms') to back new songs has gone on since reggae's inception, but, pushed to extremes, it can only harm sales. Most people agree that the point of no return is nearing.

And yet, undeterred by this general malaise, certain singers are going from strength to strength. Experienced artists like Dennis Brown, Gregory Isaacs and Sugar Minott continue to make intelligent, eminently accessible reggae; newcomers like Ini Kamoze, Michael Prophet and Frankie Paul prove that Jamaica's celebrated vocal tradition is in safe hands, while a host of DJs (or 'toasters' as they were once called) line up to follow albino superstar Yellow Man onto the rhythm tracks of currently popular songs. In Britain, groups such as Aswad and Steel Pulse are busy exploiting a more catholic range of musical influences to create a genuinely progressive strain of reggae, that nods in the direction of any number of other popular forms. Armed with a stoical determination that is as much a defence mechanism as a sign of moral perfection, reggae's vanguard soldiers on, awaiting the day when the barriers come down, and the press and radio barons open the door and let reggae in from the cold.

But will it happen? Ali Campbell of UB40 (one of the few bands to achieve superstar status via Jamaican rhythms) may earnestly declare *"Right now, reggae music is what the people want"*, but do they? Reggae flourished in the era of punk, when its

● Peter Tosh

● Bob Marley

militantly anti-imperialistic sentiments chimed in harmoniously with the prevailing vogue for iconoclastic nose-thumbing, but as the recession has bitten harder, the kids have clamoured for songs that offer a fantasy escape from, rather than reminders of, the problems of contemporary urban living. Jamaican music, throughout its passage from home-grown R'n'B to fevered ska, romantic, chugging rocksteady and finally to reggae, has always invoked the imagery of shanty town life and hard, unrewarding work. To most pop fans, Club Tropicana or Rio seem more attractive than the Trenchtown ghetto or the Spanish Town Road. Dreams are marketable; evocations of harsh reality have an irksome tendency to stay on the shop shelf.

In this respect, reggae's loss of favour has benefitted other ethnic music. Aside from Errol and his ilk, much of reggae's audience comprises middle class white youths with a taste for the mildly exotic and a wage that permits freelance exploration of the latest imported music fad. This 'next big thing' factor has played no small part in the recent boom in sales of African and Latin records, with many erstwhile reggae fans transferring their allegiance to lighter, more celebratory sounds. Even soca — another established Caribbean music, but one that blends soul and calypso to yield a furious dance beat — has made great popular progress. Arrow's **Hot! Hot! Hot!** was a dancefloor smash in 1983, and at growing numbers of 'radical dance' clubs across the country it's virtually *de rigeur* to slot some freshly-acquired Barbadian release into the procedings somewhere. Expect the trendiest Camden parties to reverberate to the pulse of Aborigine rain-cycle chants any day now…

Pessimistic, even cynical as this outlook may seem, reggae and ethnic music generally will continue to repay the curiosity of the adventurous. If one feature sets them aside from the mainstream of pop, to which they offer such a refreshing alternative, it is this: these are types of music which develop by the force of experiment, held in check by the discipline of tradition. The whims or schemes of producers and executives with an eye for the main chance have played little part in their progress to date, and are unlikely to do so in the future. Investigate and you'll hear music stripped of the hype and hoo-hah, and reinstated as a simple aural and spiritual pleasure.

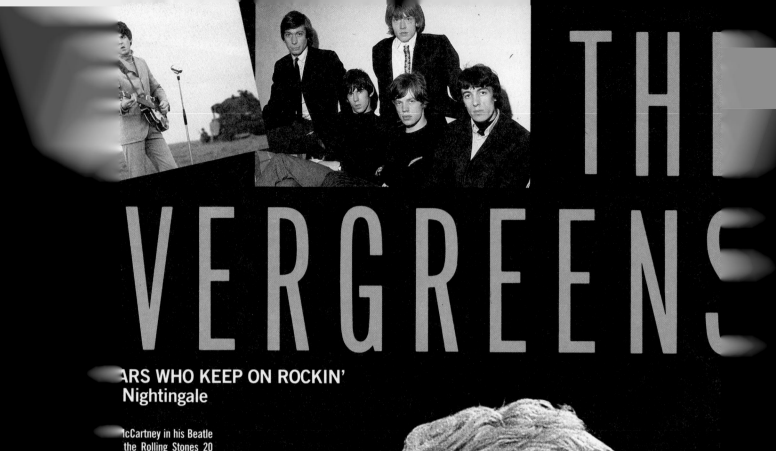

THE
VERGREENS

ARS WHO KEEP ON ROCKIN'
Nightingale

IcCartney in his Beatle
the Rolling Stones 20
. Right: David Bowie in
nation.

At the end of the sixties as the Beatles broke up, it was naturally assumed that there would be another group to follow who would be as phenomenally successful and influential as they had been. The Rolling Stones now had their place, with Jagger firmly established as the arch-duke of rock. But they always knew they had been an alternative to the Beatles, and Jagger has admitted that without the Beatles, the Stones might not ever have become a force at all. From him, some admission. So where was this new phenomenon going to come from? The assumption was never questioned. Eventually the horrible truth dawned. It *wasn't* going to happen again. There would not be another group from somewhere in the provinces of Britain who would become the four most famous people in the world.

But given that there had been *some* musical phenomenon dominating each decade before the Beatles, viz Crosby, Sinatra and Presley, then surely there must be someone on the horizon.

It turned out to be David Bowie, although he took his time. His first hit took SIX YEARS to reach Number One ! But once he'd changed his name from Jones, he proved to be the most different. Dashing and shocking, he took the androgynous theme much further than Jagger had dared to do. Musically his influence has been infinite. But for years it was subtle and unseen. Bowie was busy confusing his audience by constantly changing his style and persona. He even retired. But after a decade of his chameleon-like behaviour, by 1983 he had established himself as the world's most influential rock performer. He had now proved himself to be a lasting influence, particularly on other musicians. He has always striven for change and experimentation, and consequently stayed in front. Perhaps it has to do with his environment. Bowie has never 'settled' anywhere. His base may be Switzerland, but he'll turn up anywhere from Berlin to Brighton, New York to Tokyo, taking up the influence of his surroundings.

It's one way of doing it. Another is to stay determinedly British, like Status Quo and Slade have done. From the early Quo days of the rather surreal and psychedelic **Pictures Of Matchstick Men** and **Ice In The Sun**, they stumbled on that hard driving style — which gave them their first Number One with **Down Down** — and stuck to it. Status Quo's longevity relied on exactly the opposite requirement of Bowie. In the ever shifting music world, one looked to Quo *not* to alter. Had they ditched their jeans in 1977 and turned punk, all would have been lost.

The story is even truer of Slade, who could survive for six months in the Antarctic with half a bar of chocolate between them, such is their resilience. And exuberance. Their classic anthem, **Merry Christmas Everybody,** has been a hit for Slade no less than four times. The most notable performance of the song being at the Reading Festival on August bank holiday! At that time their popularity had dwindled, to such an extent that they were booked as a last minute replacement at the Festival. But they still managed to steal the show. Even in the age of mini-epic videos, nothing can quite match the ability of Slade to create sheer enjoyment in live performance. There is nothing particularly artistically innovative about Slade, but they have a unique ability to bring a smile to the face.

Innovation has been left to bands like Roxy Music. Their style has left its mark on many a band of the eighties. John Taylor, bass player with Duran Duran, claims to know everything there is to know about Roxy Music, such was their influence on *him*. Roxy was all about style. And timing. They

appeared literally from nowhere in 1972, when popular music was in one of its periodic sloughs. That year had seen such memorable hits as **Mother Of Mine** by Neil Reid, **Come What May** by Vicky Leandros and **Could It Be Forever** from David Cassidy. Roxy came along and happened within a week. They 'dressed' their first album sleeve like no one had ever bothered to do before, they looked extraordinary and most importantly of all their musical style was original. Bryan Ferry, who clipped away at his Geordie accent till he sounded like Prince Charles, had the forceful determination to be a star. One aspect of the band's ability could have been enhanced had Brian Eno stayed with Roxy Music. But his clashes with Ferry made him leave. A pity. Eno's experimental talent would have pushed Roxy Music further forward musically had he stayed with them.

● More grand old men of rock: (from top to bottom) Slade, Roxy Music and Status Quo.

● They just keep on rockin': (from top right) Rod Stewart, Bruce Springsteen, Queen.

● Above: Eric Clapton
Inset: Phil Collins

Genesis' survival tactics are the more remarkable because they came out of the rock genre which took itself seriously enough to have earned the tag 'pomp-rock'. The late sixties and early seventies had bred in Britain all too many groups in this category and seemed to attract a following of people who really wanted to hear safe, unthreatening 'light' music, verging on a quasi-classical style. When Peter Gabriel, the visual lynch-pin of Genesis quit the band, Genesis was virtually written off. But no one had reckoned with the staying power, energy and talent of Phil Collins. For a drummer to come from the back and take over the leadership of a group was pretty well unheard of. And paring the group down seemed to give them a new vitality, and strangely too, Genesis held their hard core of fans with an almost devoted loyalty. Now the only cloud on their horizon appears to be the amount of solo success which has come Phil Collins' way. It raised the question of how long he will want to stay within the group. But Collins, by his own admission is a workaholic, happy to plunge himself into as many musical projects as he has time for, whether it be producing Adam Ant or Eric Clapton…

Clapton's own career over the past few years has been low profile but resolute. He lived uncomfortably through the sixties with his nickname 'God', the most idolised guitarist of his generation. The mantle took its toll, and Eric was beset with dependence on drugs and alcohol. He has never enjoyed being the front man centre stage and although he acknowledges a star's ego, it never prevented him from wanting to share his music with the very best musicians he could find to work with. For several years he took almost a back seat with his playing and stage performances. Musically he has mellowed, and is no longer interested in playing fast flashy solos. His most successful material has turned out to be love songs – particularly **Layla** and **Wonderful Tonight.** But he insists that he is not often visited by the inspiration which creates classic songs. And adds that he's not very sure that he would want to be! Each year he has a heavy international touring schedule and contrives to keep his music fresh by changing his backing bands fairly regularly. Presumably he will go on for ever.

Concerning Bruce Springsteen there are just two very definitely split camps. Those who believe he is the saviour of rock'n'roll, and those who do not. From the beginning, Springsteen was the subject of a heavy American publicity machine, which made suspicious British audiences smell hype. His reputation never really recovered from this, which makes assessing his real worth a hazy question. For those who have hailed Bruce as the saviour, it is his emotional street cred which has created the appeal. And no one would deny that his anything-up-to-four-hour stage performances have been spectacular. It is also true that he is the only white American rock superstar which that country has produced in more than a decade. And Americans love heroes.

Although he was selling out the Wembley arena at the turn of the decade, no one took much notice of Billy Joel until he started dating top model Christie Brinkley. Joel's career has been full of ups and downs ever since his days playing favourite tunes for drunks in piano bars. His marriage to Elizabeth – who took control of his career – inspired albums like **The Stranger** and songs like **Just The Way You Are,** but after that collapsed, Christie and his love for early sixties pop songs culminated in **Innocent Man,** a Number One with **Uptown Girl,** a live BBC broadcast for his Wembley shows and no less than five albums in the charts. Not bad for a self-confessed ugly shortarse with a penchant for playing the piano.

Queen's main claim to fame will always revolve around **Bohemian Rhapsody,** which stayed at the top of the charts for nine weeks and became the first hit acknowledged to have been enhanced by the accompanying video. The split screen and other effects used helped the record sustain its success and proved fairly conclusively that a good video could sell a record. The flamboyant Freddie Mercury has led Queen from one dramatic theatrical stance to another. It was clear from the start of Queen's career that they had musicianship on their side, but it has been Mercury's tricks and camp outrageousness which has kept them interesting.

It is also showmanship which has kept Rod Stewart's flame afire, despite some rather serious lulls and unproductive periods. At worst he can cut a ludicrous figure, pouting, posing and posturing on stage, looking embarrassingly foolish. At best he's a superb entertainer in front of a stadium full of fans. The foghorn voice has not let him down and many times he has proved he has a talent which most music publishers would envy him. That is an ability to spot a hit song when he hears one. **Maggie May** and **Sailing** are both cases in point. It is this commercial shrewdness, not his hairstyle which has kept Rod Stewart going.

With John Lennon dead, Ringo Starr more interested in film acting and George Harrison more interested in film making, Paul McCartney is the only Beatle left still making music for a living. He has of course been accused of being bland, trite and sentimental. Clearly his song writing style

THE EVERGREENS

EVERGREENS

● More golden oldies: Elton John (left), Bob Dylan (top) and Roger Daltrey (below)

changed after the Lennon-McCartney partnership broke up, since then McCartney's lyrics have not possessed the edge that was clearly Lennon's influence. And yet... Paul McCartney's ability to create a memorable melody line apparently effortlessly is extraordinary. He is prolific — perhaps too prolific — and in the rather lonely job of being Paul McCartney his difficulty appears to be in finding objectivity in his own music. If he can be persuaded to go out on the road again he will be able to demonstrate his incredible grasp of stage dynamics. His world tour with Wings remains one of the best live rock shows ever seen.

If rock'n'roll had never been invented there still would have been Elton John. His desire to entertain would have burst forth on whatever had been the music style of the day. In fact he has never been part of any fashion genre within popular music, and nor has he ever needed to be. His songs have immense staying power, and the best don't date at all. **Your Song**, his very first hit, is as fresh today as when it was recorded in 1971. Elton's great strength is in writing intensely personal songs with

which his audiences can identify, almost passionately.

It is a sense of mystery too, which has always surrounded Bob Dylan. His influence could never be minimised and his uncanny prophetic qualities stand for all time. Yet his changes in style and attitude are bewildering, and leave his audience unsure how to respond to him. Songs with social conscience give way to love ballads, and then switch back again. His droney voice is regarded as mesmerising by some, and irritating by others. Dylan remains an enigma, and it's his obvious intention to stay that way.

It will be interesting to see over the next ten years, how many of these so-called evergreens become dead leaves.

ORIGINS OF BAND NAMES AND SONG TITLES
AND OTHER FASCINATING FACTS
by Phil Swern

How many times have you looked down the charts and seen the name of a new band that makes you stop and think why did they call themselves that? How many times have you heard a new release on the radio and know you've heard that song somewhere before? Maybe the song title itself is a phrase that you've heard time and time again, but can't remember where.

Can you imagine a band naming themselves after the gurgling of a new born baby? Well that's how Kajagoogoo arrived at their name. Who would have thought a Doris Day hit from 1964 would find its way back into the charts in 1983? Tracey Ullman managed to achieve a top ten hit with the title song of one of Doris' movies, *Move Over, Darling.* Another movie connection can be found in the title of the first solo hit for Nick Heyward after leaving Haircut 100. It was called **Whistle Down The Wind,** which was the title of a 1961 film starring Hayley Mills. *The Night Has A Thousand Eyes* was a 1948 movie starring Edward G. Robinson and a 1963 top ten hit for Bobby Vee.

Blue Monday by New Order was in and out of the British charts like a yo-yo for many months from 1983-4. The song, of course, was original, as far as for the title, well, way back in 1957, Fats Domino was climbing the British charts with a completely different song, though the title was the same.

Let's look at a few more movie links. Back in 1965, a group called Them had two hits with **Baby Please Don't Go,** and **Here Comes The Night.** Their name was derived from a very nasty film from 1954 about atomic bomb radiation causing giant ants to breed in the New Mexico desert. Still in the sixties, the Searchers found their name from the title of a famous John Wayne picture, and there was a series of movies about a troubled surburban man named Dagwood Bumstead and his wife, Blondie; there's no hard evidence that the band took their name from that source, but it's a nice thought. Then there's a girl group, The Little Foxes, who are the daughters of the fifties trio, the Beverley Sisters. *The Little Foxes* was a 1941 movie starring Bette Davis.

Family ties abound in the music business. Did you know that singer-songwriter Andrew Gold is the son of Ernest, composer of many famous movie scores including **Exodus.** Randy Newman has Alfred and Lionel for uncles, both famous for their film scores. Elvis Costello is the son of Ross McManus, who was a singer with, can you believe it, the Joe Loss Orchestra; and remember Kate Robbins, who sang **More Than In Love** in *Crossroads?* Well, her cousin is none other than Paul McCartney. Lucky Paul, or lucky Kate, whichever way you care to look at it.

Paul McCartney was also inspiration for The Ramones: they took their name from Paul Ramone, a pseudonym McCartney occasionally used back in the sixties. Led Zeppelin, are so called, it is believed, because a certain member of The Who heard their music and stated that he thought the band in Britain would go down like a lead one. The name The Lotus Eaters is derived from a poem by Lord Tennyson *Song Of The Lotus Eaters:* a Lotus Eater is a person who lives in a state of constant pleasure. Whilst on the subject of Tennyson, how's this for trivia — did you know he wrote the words to that blockbuster song **Come Into The Garden Maude.**

The origins of bands' names are fascinating. Simple Minds found theirs in a line from the David

Bowie hit **The Jean Genie,** while Madness was a Prince Buster song the guys used to perform on stage. Altered Images was the name of a design company credited on the sleeve of a hit single, and The Heaven 17 was a fictitious group shown on an album sleeve in the film *Clockwork Orange.* The Rolling Stones were named after a Muddy Waters blues song; Deep Purple came from a Bing Crosby standard; and who would think of calling themselves after the code number of a dole card? UB40, that's who. Thin Lizzy is a charactor in The Bash Street Kids, a cartoon from the *Beano,* and Duran Duran was a mechanical character in the movie *Barbarella,* made in 1967 and starring Jane Fonda.

Perhaps if you'd gone to an American girls' school, it may well have been called Belle Stars; or could you ever have seen an Australian TV detective called *Boney M.* Maybe you've visited a fashion store in France called Depeche Mode, or bought an American blues record on the Yazoo label — or drowned in the river of the same name.

So what about some of those recent chart hits that are not appearing in the best sellers lists for the first time. Phil Collins had his first solo Number One hit in 1983 with **You Can't Hurry Love,** but the original by The Supremes merely reached Number Three in 1966. **Na Na, Hey Hey, Kiss Him Goodbye,** another top ten hit in 1983 for Bananarama, proved to be a one hit wonder for American group, Steam, back in 1970, and UB40's Number One hit **Red Red Wine** was originally recorded in the late sixties by the composer Neil Diamond. The song appeared briefly in the charts in 1968, when it was a minor hit for Jimmy James and the Vagabonds, and again the following year, a smaller hit still for reggae singer Tony Tribe.

Can't Get Used To Losing You, a Number Three hit for The Beat, reached Number Two in 1963 for Andy Williams. Cliff Richard's hit **True Love Ways** had been on the British charts on two other occasions, once in 1960 when the original by Buddy Holly stood at Number 23, and again in 1963 when a version by Peter and Gordon reached Number Two. Incidentally, Peter of Peter and Gordon is the brother of actress Jane Asher — it's all relative you know.

Shakin' Stevens has also been known to record the odd song or two from the archives. His first Number One, **This Ole House** was a top 30 hit in America in 1954 for its composer Stuart Hamblen, and a Number One on both sides of the Atlantic in the same year for Rosemary Clooney. Still with the same song in that same year, a British female artist named Billie Anthony climbed to the Number Four position in the UK charts. The next time Mr. Stevens made the Number One slot was with **Green Door;** the original version of that was by Jim Lowe, a UK Number Eight in 1956, also covered and taken into the charts at the same time by Frankie Vaughan, his version reaching Number Two, and a smaller hit for Glen Mason. Mr. S was recently in great shakes with a hit duet with Bonnie Tyler called **A Rockin' Good Way,** originally an American top ten hit for Brook Benton and Dinah Washington.

When the movie *Up The Junction* comes on the telly next, ask someone who had a hit record with that title? You might just be able to Squeeze it out of them, but should you find yourself in Dire Straits, just drink a large Bucks Fizz and you'll soon be Kissing the Pink.

BE A SPORT!

by Patrick MacLachlan

There's a buzz of excitement that rumbles up to a monstrous roar as the darling of the crowd steps out into the glare of the flashbulbs and lights, waving and blowing kisses all the way to the back of the bleachers.

Somehow, you always expect a megastar to look larger than life. But this bloke's so spindly, his artfully tousled mane of curls must weigh more than the rest of him put together. He looks almost lost among the supporting players and it seems inconceivable that such a slightly built figure can hold such sway over this sold-out crowd of thousands. Yet he has them screaming at every last twitch of his finger for the best part of two hours, as he enthrals them with his trademarked blend of utter professional skill and inspired creative magic.

His performance climaxes with a firework display that turns the night time city into day. The noise of it even drowns the yelling of the fans. Then,

crescendo upon crescendo, a helicopter clatters down from the sky, picks him up and bears him aloft and away, like an updated version of the Ascension Into Heaven.

Who is it? Bob Dylan at the Budokan? Michael Jackson at Madison Square Garden? No. It's Kevin Keegan at St. James's Park, playing his farewell game for Newcastle.

Apart from the adulation they receive, there are some interesting parallels between the people at the top in sport and music. Not least of them is the attraction they seem to have for each other.

Perhaps it's because they find themselves in similar situations that are equally bizarre. Because although there are some notable exceptions, it's fair to say that the majority of the leading names in pop and sport are of no more than middling intelligence and intellectual ability. It's also fair to say that if some of them had dynamite for brains,

• From top left: tennis star Vitas Gerulaitas plays an ace guitar, but it's love all for Cliff Richard on the tennis court.

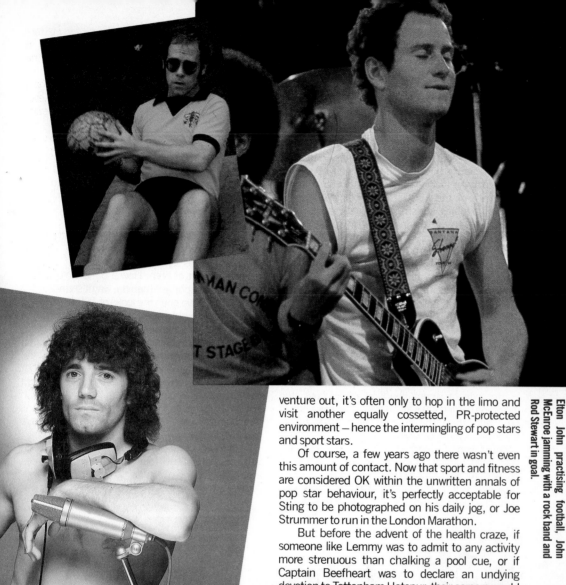

● Kevin Keegan in the recording studio, Elton John practising football, John McEnroe jamming with a rock band and Rod Stewart in goal.

BEAT A SPORT!

they wouldn't have enough to blow their hats off. If they didn't have this wonderful ability to whack pieces of leather-bound cork extremely hard with lumps of carved willow, or caress a set of taut metal strings in the right order, or whatever it is they're good at, they'd be ordinary people with ordinary lives.

But there they are, with barrowloads of fivers in the bank and their pictures grinning down from the walls of a million teenage bedrooms. When they were kids, kicking a tennis ball round the schoolyard or furtively practising their dance steps in front of the bedroom mirror, they couldn't have had the faintest idea of what they were getting into. And because it's only recently that the actual performers — instead of the middlemen in both sport and music — have started to pick up the fattest slice of the cake, there isn't even a precedent for them to follow. There aren't many people who can offer advice based on experience to these young Turks, who could be millionaires before the age of 25.

It's all uncharted territory. And I bet it's really weird. No wonder some of them go barmy and loads of them get heavily into drink, or drugs, or gambling, or anything to take the edge off the freakish unreality of their situation. And no wonder they live and socialise within a heavily guarded, hermetically sealed world. If and when they do venture out, it's often only to hop in the limo and visit another equally cossetted, PR-protected environment — hence the intermingling of pop stars and sport stars.

Of course, a few years ago there wasn't even this amount of contact. Now that sport and fitness are considered OK within the unwritten annals of pop star behaviour, it's perfectly acceptable for Sting to be photographed on his daily jog, or Joe Strummer to run in the London Marathon.

But before the advent of the health craze, if someone like Lemmy was to admit to any activity more strenuous than chalking a pool cue, or if Captain Beefheart was to declare an undying devotion to Tottenham Hotspur, their careers would be pretty well torpedoed.

Nowadays there's no holding them apart. You've got Cliff Richard canoodling in the most Christian way possible with Sue Barker, and Adam Faith — according to last year's gossip sheets — playing mixed singles with Chris Evert. You've got the likes of Elton John and Rod Stewart using their extremely expensive vocal chords for the purpose of belting out smash hits like Come On You Blues.

And if you ever study the newspapers' racing pages, you're likely to get a shock when you see occasional pictures of an immaculately dressed gent complete with trilby, tweeds and a leather binoculars case — picking up yet another trophy for one of his fabulously expensive and enormously successful race horses. Nothing at all shocking about that, of course, except that this particular sultan of the turf is none other than Eric Clapton.

Surely in the future, the two worlds will become indivisible. There are already pro-celebrity tournaments in most major sports. How long can it be before the tables are turned and we see the posters going up for An Evening With Daley Thompson And The London Philharmonic, or Bill Webernuik With Meatloaf? How long can it be before football clubs switch their format around to 90 minutes of music with a ten minute kickabout in between? Or pigeon racing becomes the country's biggest spectator sport, by the simple device of getting Ozzy Osbourne to congratulate the winning birds in his own inimitable way?

Well, why not? It's all entertainment. And if Bobby Robson played Boy George at outside right, at least we'd know for sure he wasn't serious.

IMAGE MAKERS

by Lesley-Ann Jones

Pop culture, as the record industry has been swift to realise, is big business. It is not enough, these days, to make fashionable music. That irresistible trademark of the 1980's, a preoccupation with style and things stylish, must apply across the board. The fans are buying the whole package, not just a new sound . . . and they expect value for money. They demand a new image to play with and to imitate. Identifying with the stars of the moment, to the chagrin of many parents, is a way of life. Witness the surging success of Duran Duran, Spandau Ballet, Culture Club and Wham! — then count the clones. Gone the laid-back indifference of the 'trendy' seventies, when the British monopoly of the music market was temporarily lost. Mass hysteria and hero worship, sixties style, is back — along with a healthy harvest of freshly cultivated, home-grown bands.

In spite of recent phenomenal success, the recession has left its mark on the music business as on every other. The champagne breakfasts are fewer and further between; the financial risks now being taken by record companies are well-calculated indeed. Nothing, it seems, is left to chance. All angles of the market are meticulously explored. But the business is still a hazardous tightrope for those without sufficient confidence or commitment and the suss to realise that fashions were never more shortlived. A pop band must develop almost ahead of the times, both musically and visually, if it is to survive. Any brand of excitement becomes stale, predictable and boring if it hangs around too long.

Today, it takes much more than a smattering of good songs to launch a band on the road to success. It takes style, and it takes image — and not a small amount of both. How a band looks is now almost more important than the way it sounds.

So what have been the looks of 1984? Outsized white T shirts emblazoned with poignant messages in large black lettering and dinky pairs of boxer shorts do not suit everyone. Denim has never been unpopular; it has never needed to make the dreaded comeback every few years like, say, leather or plastic. Even so, only the most established performers in the world can get away with appearing on stage in a T shirt and a pair of jeans (Rolling Stones and Police take note). The rest have to try a little harder . . .

We took a look at what musical types have been wearing, and chose four of the strongest styles around for the lovely Andrew to model. Over to you, Andrew . . .

Andrew
"What on earth have I let myself in for here? What did I do to deserve this? Turn up at Paul's studio at 10 o'clock, they said, washed and ready for make-up. An ominous selection of gawdy garments hanging on the rail here . . . what on earth are they going to *do* to me? Do I need this? Sarah the make-up artist is calling me to be made up for the first session. I can hardly wait . . ."

New Hippy/Horticultural Look (*Morrissey of the Smiths*)

"They call him the Guru of bed-sit dwellers and sulky sixth-formers — I'm beginning to see why. Adopt loose posture, they tell me. Do not fall over. Use props supplied by the House and Garden Horticultural Snatch Squad; listen carefully to **I'm so miserable now,** and try to feel like that (it's not hard, let me assure you . . .) and wonder at the horrified expression of the man with the Box Brownie.

"The clothes? — colourful shirts, open to the waist, tied or tucked; faded jeans, no shoes, beads and botanical accessories."

Clothes supplied by American Classics, 404 Kings Road, London SW3.
Necklaces: junk shop selection.

Total look: approx £30.

Go Western (*as flirted with by the likes of Icicle Works, Bluebells, The Alarm, Aztec Camera and Yip Yip Coyote*)

"No one can give me a good answer as to who wears this sort of thing in rock music today. I'll just have to trust them! However, doubts aside, great jacket — feels good on, induces childhood regression, urban wigwam, 45.46-litre hats etc. The boots are very comfortable, until you try to stand up and walk. This is probably because the heels are a good few minutes ahead of the toes. The only way to maintain a vertical stance is to adopt the cowboy walk — which all goes to prove that cobblers have a highly developed sense of humour.

"Paul the photographer wants to cut my head off in this one."

Clothes supplied by Johnsons, 406 Kings Road, London SW3.

Total look: approx £320.

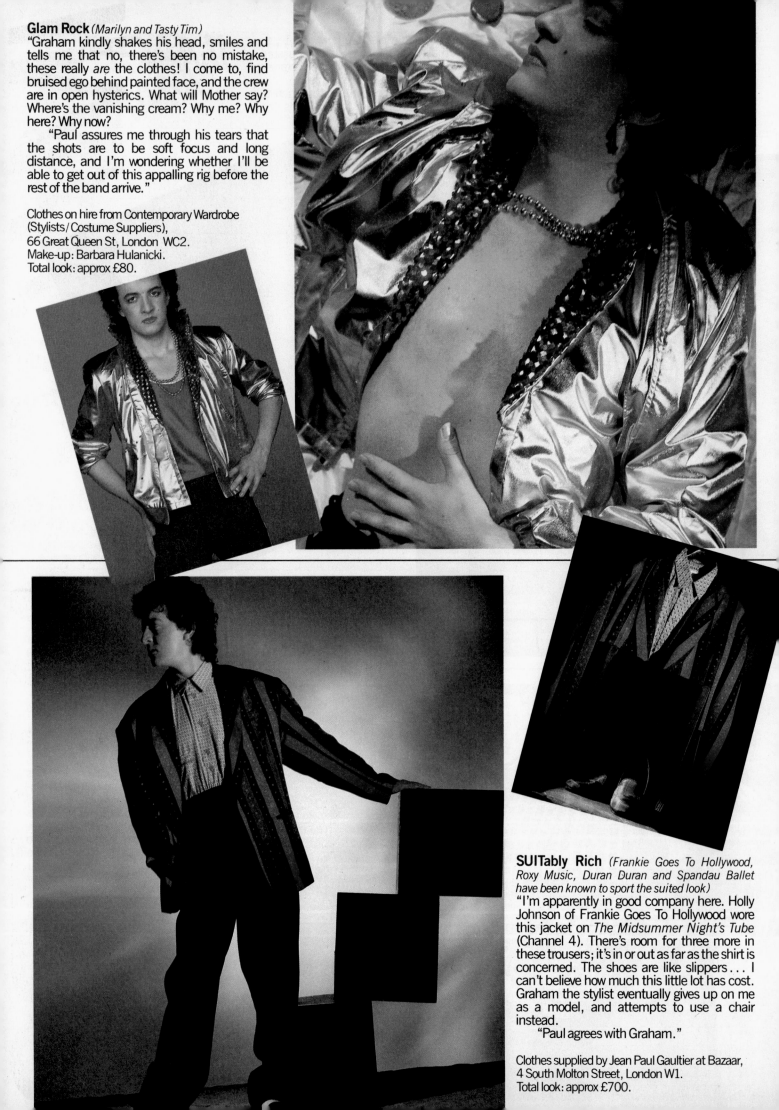

Glam Rock *(Marilyn and Tasty Tim)*

"Graham kindly shakes his head, smiles and tells me that no, there's been no mistake, these really *are* the clothes! I come to, find bruised ego behind painted face, and the crew are in open hysterics. What will Mother say? Where's the vanishing cream? Why me? Why here? Why now?

"Paul assures me through his tears that the shots are to be soft focus and long distance, and I'm wondering whether I'll be able to get out of this appalling rig before the rest of the band arrive."

Clothes on hire from Contemporary Wardrobe (Stylists / Costume Suppliers),
66 Great Queen St, London WC2.
Make-up: Barbara Hulanicki.
Total look: approx £80.

SUITably Rich *(Frankie Goes To Hollywood, Roxy Music, Duran Duran and Spandau Ballet have been known to sport the suited look)*

"I'm apparently in good company here. Holly Johnson of Frankie Goes To Hollywood wore this jacket on *The Midsummer Night's Tube* (Channel 4). There's room for three more in these trousers; it's in or out as far as the shirt is concerned. The shoes are like slippers . . . I can't believe how much this little lot has cost. Graham the stylist eventually gives up on me as a model, and attempts to use a chair instead.

"Paul agrees with Graham."

Clothes supplied by Jean Paul Gaultier at Bazaar, 4 South Molton Street, London W1.
Total look: approx £700.

THE IMAGEMAKERS ARE:
Stylist: Graham K. Smith
Make-up: Sarah Matheson
Photography: Paul Cox

Conclusion: Andrew
"Yes . . . all very well, and I've learned a lot today — but I can't really see myself in any of this lot. Must sit down and talk it over with the band."

KALOO KALAY
are a brand new band: watch this space!

They are (from left to right) Steve Roberts, Andrew McGillivray, John Davies and James Browne.

"What's in a name?" says Andrew. "Well, everything and nothing. The name and the music are inspired by various literary and musical disciplines. The band's theme song **Kaloo Kalay** itself reflects these influences, and the lyrics speak for themselves.

"We are rhythm, Soundyway, Scoldyblueface, Kaloo Kalay."

Kaloo Kalay: Clothes supplied by Wendy Dagworthy and Katharine Hamnett; styled by Olivia Komlosy. Hair by Martin Unerman at John Frieda.

PRODUCER STEVE LEVINE – THE MAN AND HIS WORK

Lesley-Ann Jones

In a curiously drab and uninteresting corner of north-west London, an unobtrusive building crouches apologetically behind the mock-Tudor public conveniences. Its brass door plate is engraved with the words RED BUS, and the reception area is like Doctor Who's tardis: how did such a small exterior suddenly become so spacious? Plenty of people are hard at work in this, one of London's finest and best-equipped recording studios; not least a tall, dark and dangerously handsome 26-year-old who goes by the name of Steve Levine and who, early in 1984, received two major awards in the space of a few days (from the B.P.I. and Music Week) for Best Producer, 1983. But Steve Levine is not a man to rest on his laurels — far from it. Currently one of the most sought-after producers in town (the industry term is 'hot'), he has, to date, worked on everything by Culture Club, including the latest album; with Bob Marley's children, the charming Melody Makers, in Jamaica; and back in the Red Bus studios with none other than the Beach Boys — who, incidentally, have never all recorded together on an album until now.

Impressive achievements indeed for one so young — but Levine didn't get where he is today without putting the hours in. When he left school, he had no musical experience whatsoever. He did the only thing he could do — start at the bottom.

"I didn't actually want to be a producer when I was at school", he says, taking a break at the mixing console and reaching for an apple and a cup of tea.

"To be honest, I didn't really know what one was! But I'd always liked electronics. I made a discotheque while I was still at school, and I soon decided that I wanted to make records. I suppose I was about 13 when I first set my sights on a job in the music industry."

At 17 he arrived at the CBS studios with no experience and little knowledge. His first job was as a tape operator working on demos for new bands. It was producer Bruce Johnson who first hired him as an engineer. Impressed by Steve's aptitude and enthusiasm, he took him to Los Angeles to work on some recordings, and encouraged him to become a producer himself.

"By that time I'd already decided that it was the job for me", recalls Steve. "In the studio, the producer is boss; that suited me down to the ground."

Back in London, he dabbled in several projects, some of which were successful and others not, before signing a deal with Rondor Music which supplied him with enough money to buy a Linn Drum Computer. It was one of the first ever in the country, and it quickly became part of the 'Steve Levine Sound'.

In 1981, he was approached by a completely unknown group of musicians who asked him to work on their demos. They had a great image and some exciting ideas up their sleeves, but they needed somebody to be 'in charge' — someone who could pull it all together. After a shaky start, the band were signed by Virgin Records, and Steve set about turning the best song of their first proper session into a hit. **Do You Really Want To Hurt Me** shot to Number One in the UK charts. The success of Culture Club was assured.

Offers were soon flooding in, and since then he has worked with Jimmy the Hoover, David Grant and the larger-than-life Helen Terry. He has also been making some rather fine music of his own — not bad for a man who was never taught to play a musical instrument.

"No, I never had piano lessons or anything like that, and I still wouldn't know where to start with a guitar. I acquired my knowledge out of necessity, and gradually picked up on the keyboards to get a feel for what my musicians were doing. It whetted my appetite to do something more."

In February 1984 he signed a recording contract with Chrysalis Records, who issued his first single **Believin' It All** in March. Co-written by Boy George, it featured John Alder on lead vocals, and included the Melody Makers' mum, Rita Marley, on backing vocals.

"Because the record said 'by Steve Levine', quite a few people did assume it was me singing at first", he laughs. "But I don't know why they should jump to such conclusions. Van Halen doesn't sing, and neither does Spandau Ballet's Gary Kemp. And let's face it, they wouldn't be a band without him. I may well sing on a track one day. But I'm an ardent fan of vocals. I can enjoy someone else's voice much more than my own."

His first album **Across The Board** was also co-written with a selection of artistes.

"I wrote two with Colin Blunstone, a couple with John Alder, and Boy George collaborated on two as well. George is a media dream. Not only is he great to work with, he's also one of the most marketable people in the industry. His name on my album can't do any harm at all."

So what, in layman's terms, does a producer do?

"I wish I had a pound for every time I've heard that question asked!" laughs Steve.

"In the old days, there was no such term. Veterans like Beatles producer George Martin were called Artistes and Recording Managers — and they did everything under the sun. They decided on all the arrangements and even told the boys what to wear! But the record industry has come a long way since then — thank God. I suppose as a producer, I'm responsible for the final product — what the finished record will sound like. But every

● Steve in control

● A great team — Steve with Culture Club

producer has his own way of achieving that. There's no right or wrong way of doing it; we all find our own style. Having said that, it's a dangerous thing to become too recognisable in terms of sound. It restricts you terribly — and it limits your range.

"Not all producers come up through engineering like I did, but it certainly helps. I'm quite technically minded. I know how to get the sounds I want. The relationship between producer and engineer is very important — equally as precious as that between producer and artiste. It's vital that we are all sympathetic to each other's problems. After that, it's anybody's guess! The starting point varies according to who you're working with. Culture Club, for example, don't do demo tapes. They have a quick rehearsal and then bash out their rough ideas onto a Walkman. It's all very raw — a bar length and a bit of melody — but then we go into the studio and build it up as we go along. All their ideas are developed in the studio. It works for them, but not for everyone. David Grant's material is demo'd almost to a finished level at times.

"I'd rather start from scratch any day. Demos can be harmful.

"It's also my job to look for back-up musicians and vocalists; decide on equipment, arrange dates — you name it. As far as the live-ware is concerned, we all have people we like to work with. It's very important to create a good working environment and help the artiste to feel secure in his surroundings.

"Above all, it's my job to find out what the artiste wants the song to sound like; incorporate my own ideas without being overpowering; bring out the best in him, and capture his finest performance on tape without in any way cramping his style. You must be able to inspire him to do great things without being too interfering! Sounds

impossible? It sometimes is! I suppose you also need great imagination — the sensitivity to know when to call it a day. Overproduction can be worse than none at all."

Studio conversation is peppered with peculiar words like 'outboard', 'groove', 'reverb', 'sequencing', 'noise gates', 'overdub' and 'roll-off'.

"Don't be put off by technical jargon" grins Steve.

"We know what we're talking about."

Glad he does.

He is the proud possessor of a SONY PCM 3324 24-track digital tape machine, for which he paid in the region of £110,000. It was the first of its kind in Britain —

"... and it's the reason I don't have a huge mansion in the country! I've put my money to good use. In fact, all the equipment in this particular studio belongs to me. The only thing which remains the property of Red Bus is the desk! I've customised the control room to suit my needs, and absolutely nobody else uses it. You develop relationships with machines too, you see. I have the knowledge to programme everything I use. I also do the mixing and cutting myself. I usually cut at CBS studios; the quality is excellent, and they also have digital playback."

'Make hay while the sun shines' is Steve Levine's motto. At the moment he spends 'most of his life' in the studio, but believes it will pay dividends in the end.

"I want my own studio one day, and eventually to be able to work on one or two enormous projects of my choosing a year. I've been in a recording studio virtually every day for the past nine years — and I'm still working six or seven days a week. I couldn't physically keep up this pace forever.

"I'd like to have a family and become a normal human being one day!"

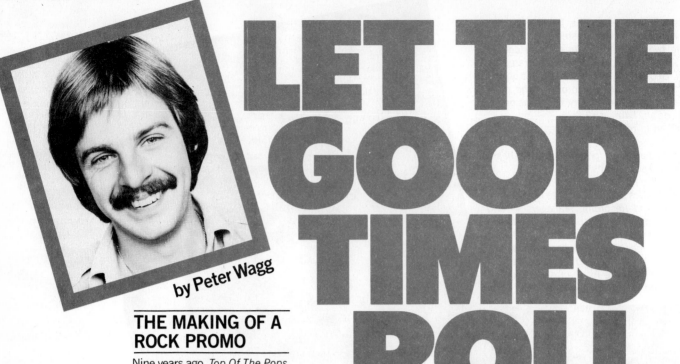

LET THE GOOD TIMES ROLL

by Peter Wagg

THE MAKING OF A ROCK PROMO

Nine years ago, *Top Of The Pops* screened a music video for a song languishing in the bottom half of the charts. It was by a group called Queen and the track was **Bohemian Rhapsody.**

It was the first time the general public had been exposed to the creative use of video applied to music. The effect was, to say the least, dramatic. After just one showing, the record shot up the charts and occupied the Number One position for an incredible nine weeks. As a result, Queen became a household name, Bruce Gowers the director became an industry name and record companies discovered a new and potent promotional device. The first creative music promo had been born.

So why was it so special? For five basic reasons. Firstly, the approach was original and people talked about it. Secondly, it was a great song — quoting an old record industry expression, *"it was in the grooves"*. Thirdly, the visual interpretation enhanced the music and the lyrics, providing instant access to a complicated rock opera sound. Fourthly, you could see all the images of the video in the mind every time the record was played: the music was brought to life. And lastly, the group were presented in a strong way.

We producers all try to capture these five basic elements in every production, but of course it very rarely happens. Classic songs, charismatic performers and creative inspiration collide all too infrequently.

The next time it happened was in David Bowie's **Ashes to Ashes.** Directed by David Mal-

● Queen in their Bohemian Rhapsody days

let, it pushed video capabilities to the full and illustrated how a series of unrelated images can be held together for three and a half hypnotic minutes by the sheer force of one personality.

But, it was at this point that the style and importance of promos perceptibly changed.

A new wave of music swept the country. Taking over from the punks came the New Romantics with their integration of fashion, image and music.

Up to this point 'visual' artists were the exception; now they were the norm. Promo clips became essential for an international market place that did not have the benefit of the mass UK domestic exposure.

Film began to dominate video, even though post production was still carried out on tape for reasons of speed. It was a perfect marriage, using the best of the traditional craft with the new technology.

The sometimes harsh and totally 'real' look of tape gave way to the softer more 'grainy' quality of film. Studio sets were discarded for locations and a new art form was created. New directors like Russell Mulcahy, Steve Barron, Godley and Creme (formerly of 10cc), and Brian Grant grasped the opportunity to cut their teeth in a new medium, where they could quite

literally throw away the rule books and write a new language in pictures.

The creative process had also changed. This new wave of musicians were very conscious of the style they were creating, and the power of the screen. To them, pictures and music went hand in glove. Consequently they would arrive with ideas for album sleeves and promos, just like they did for stage clothes and sets.

For producers and directors it was a breath of fresh air. It gave more time and energy to shape, develop and structure the idea.

This process is probably best exemplified by the most influential promo of the period **Vienna.** It marked the highpoint of a fruitful collaboration between Ultravox and Russell Mulcahy (not forgetting their producer Lexi Godfrey, who made it all happen). The fusion of sensi-

Nine years ago, Top Of The Pops screened a music video for a song languishing in the bottom half of the charts. It was by a little known group called Queen and the track was Bohemian Rhapsody.

● Vienna and Ultravox

LET THE GOOD TIMES ROLL

tive cinematic visuals and a classic song produced what to most people is a landmark in the promo's evolution. It most successfully introduced a narrative film approach that had all the essential ingredients.

The film was shot over two very long days, involving several locations in London and Vienna. The screen was clipped to suggest a feature film format and then photographed in monochrome, changing to full colour at dramatic moments.

By today's standards the budget was amazingly small for the work involved. It was delivered just eight days after our first meeting and was probably very influential in returning Ultravox their first platinum album. My only regret is that we had to edit out a scene with a Tarantula spider (the one used in the James Bond movie, *Dr No*). No doubt the original version will turn up at some time on a video cassette.

Since **Vienna**, the pop promo has come of age, with more productions, larger budgets and happily more opportunities for them to be seen. But with this, the creative freedom has gone and, all too often, so has the fun.

The emergence in the States of MTV, the 24-hour music station, has had a dramatic effect on the industry. By simply rotating promos to an ever increasing list of subscribers, they are breaking new acts.

Adam Ant, Duran Duran, Culture Club and many more can thank MTV for their successful launch in America.

Consequently, there is much more pressure and attention being focussed on the promo than ever before. This is tending to stifle creativity, because more people are getting involved. It is reminiscent of the committee who set out to design a greyhound and came up with a camel.

It is surprising that so many gems are produced when you consider the restrictions on the director. The music, the lyrics and the artist are all predetermined. The budgets are small compared to the production values and content, plus the delivery and pre-production times are virtually non-existent. They also have to please the record company, the manager, say five group members and, more often than not, the lead singer's girlfriend.

Fortunately, however, new directors are coming through to meet the challenge. Godley and Creme continue to dominate with very original and creative ideas. Their controversial **Two Tribes**, for Frankie Goes To Hollywood, may stimulate a new interest and approach. And Rocky Morton and Annabel Jankel, by their skilled integration of live action and animation, are also injecting a fresh impetus of ideas and creativity. Let the good times roll!

• Two Tribes

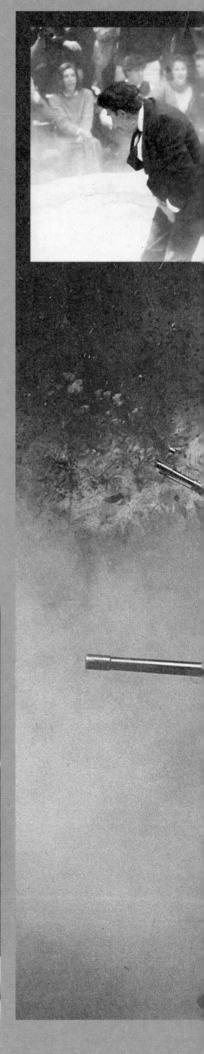

THE PACKAGING OF POP

● Kasper de Graaf talks to Malcolm Garrett

● Change of image for Yes: Malcolm Garrett's 1984 sleeve design (left) is light years away from Roger Dean's 1980 cover

Are record sleeves *that* important? It's a question that's often been asked since The Beatles made commercial art respectable by using fine artists of the day to produce cover visuals. In the seventies, illustrator Roger Dean and photographers Hipgnosis took the idea of treating the sleeve as a canvas to logical extremes. The cardboard package was seen as merely a vehicle for pictorial imagery. Although their efforts produced grand visionary works that still evoke the sounds of Yes, Led Zeppelin or Pink Floyd, the rebirth of pop in the eighties has seen the emergence of a new kind of cover art. Graphic designers have introduced a different attitude to pop packaging and marketing. How do you produce images that come to represent a band to its fans? I talked to Malcolm Garrett, whose Assorted iMaGes studio is responsible for the sleeves of many bands including Duran Duran, Culture Club, the new Yes and Simple Minds, and asked him why bands work with graphic designers.

MG: Why *do* they or why *should* they?

Why do they? Why does a band use a graphic designer?

MG: In an ideal world or the real world?

In the real world.

MG: To make money.

But what does a band need? A manager, a record company, a producer — why do they need you? Why can't the record company just put it all together and sling it out into the market?

MG: Because the record company is not fully equipped. They're not necessarily in tune with what the band are doing worldwide and in lots of other fields. Record companies are set up to distribute records. They're not set up to market and merchandise a band. They've got to deal with a whole pile of other bands as well. People who work for record companies work for record companies. I work first and foremost for the band.

How does a band go about finding a designer?

MG: I don't know, I've never tried to find one.

Well, how do bands find you then? Or how do you find bands?

MG: Either by seeing the work I've done, meeting me, being recommended to me by record companies, or by mutual contacts — that probably about covers it.

Have you ever gone out to try and get a band to work with you?

MG: If there's been some hint that a particular band were interested in working with me, and I've reciprocated that hint, then obviously I'll go out of my way to further the chance of that happening. But I haven't ever thought, I must work for this person and followed it up — it's not in my temperament.

Does the graphic designer help to sell records?

MG: Yes, inasmuch as if he's doing his job properly, he ensures that every aspect of the band's output appears to be coming from the same source, thereby reinforcing the whole feel of what's going on. So the designer may not help sell a particular record at a particular time, but he helps sell records just by enriching that general ambience about the group. He can help sell by projecting product recognition and reinforcing ideas.

What kind of link is there between the visual impression created by the designer working for the band and the music? The band is a unit that makes music, and the fans are interested in that music.

MG: But it's not just music in reality. The fans are also, for example, interested in what the musicians look like — and that's not just a question of photography, it's a question of presentation of photography. So just on a simple level, a David Levine photograph of Boy George will say one thing, but it does not say as much about George's character as David Levine's photograph of Boy George in the context of a Culture Club graphic presentation. And from the graphics you sometimes get overspill back into George's clothes. The whole design process is a constant feeding backwards and forwards of themes and ideas; so it's very difficult to actually pinpoint and say, ah, that's design, that's what happens . . . Because it's just a constant process.

Take the sleeves for Seven And The Ragged Tiger **(Duran Duran), and** Colour By Numbers **(Culture Club), and** Sparkle In The Rain **(Simple Minds). They reflect the different personalities of different bands . . .**

MG: Yes. The thing is that a designer is not really an artist *per se*. An artist is putting forward his own character and his own thoughts. A designer is putting forward his visual interpretations of his client. Therefore **Colour By Numbers, Seven And The Ragged Tiger, Sparkle In The Rain,** each of those sleeves — although they emanated from the one studio and were constructed by the one team of designers, none of the thoughts or themes displayed there are personal thoughts or themes that we're trying to push forward regardless of their relevance. We're not trying to push Assorted iMaGes as the thing that's being sold.

If an artist is like an author of ideas, doing the same as a novelist, then the designer is more like an interpreter, a translator.

MG: With a hint of copywriter, and a hint of scriptwriter, a hint of journalist, and a hint of technical writer. There's all sorts of aspects of writing that an author does not necessarily involve himself in in order to create his product. Likewise, there's a whole range of artistic activities that an artist doesn't cover.

The designer puts things together.

MG: The designer puts things together. Word-processor, thought-processor, art-processor, information-processor. Some of the things may be thoughts or ideas that have come from his own head . . .

Originated by the designer as artist.

MG: . . .or they may be originated by the band, or management . . . That's where the role of interpreter comes along. Because you've got to be able to try and work out what a 'non-visually-aware' person is trying to describe. Quite often what happens is he describes one thing and means something completely different, so you have to work out what it is that's actually being said. Or the ideas may come from the record company — there's always a lot of

● Colour By Numbers (front) . Below: the reverse side

record company pressure, which is usually of a 'commercial' nature. But they tend to forget that what is actually commercial is what's ideologically correct for the client. I was arguing with CBS Records this morning, because they wanted to see the word 'King' in 98 point, separated nice and clearly from the photographic image, where in actual fact the feel of the poster in question would then be completely changed. The feel of it would be more like a CBS poster than a King poster. You've got to sell the whole concept of beans before you can sell a single tin.

What do you think makes a good relationship between a graphic designer and a band?

MG: Contact, enthusiasm, passage of information, feedback, maintaining awareness of what's happening, what needs to happen, what hasn't happened. A designer cannot work effectively in a vacuum, because he'll end up working for himself and not for his client. He needs always to be fully briefed by the client, which doesn't necessarily mean the client telling him what to do, but it does mean the client talking to him and telling him what he himself is doing or wants to do.

Some clients are more aware of what they actually want to see than others, aren't they? How do you deal with that?

MG: Well, Boy George comes in and invariably has the photography he wants to use. He tells you what the song is about, he tells you either what the feel of the song is about or the feel of what he's trying to

● Pink Floyd's Dark Side Of The Moon

say about the world in general at that point. He dumps it all on you, says what he thinks, goes away and lets you get on with it. Brilliant. Because he's giving you *all* the information you need to do the job, and he's giving you all the faith and trust that you're actually going to do the job for him. So you actually do it.

If somebody's constantly worried about it and looking over your shoulder and changing his mind, then you just never get the job done. Because you're either never sure what to do, or if you are sure what to do, you think the man's such an arsehole he's not gonna like it, so you end up trying to please him rather than trying to do what's right. You're employed to do what's right, which isn't always something that the client can see until it's done. So if you only try and please them, try and do what they think they want, only what *they* can see, then you're probably underachieving.

Duran Duran on the other hand always tend to spur one on to overachieve. Because they have such grandiose thoughts and schemes and plans for doing things. They don't acknowledge obstacles. They just say, well, yeah, we think we should get a tiger on this one. And ordinarily you'd go, oh god, where the hell am I going to get a tiger from? But then they get a tiger, you know. Duran are very inspiring, not because they're necessarily lavish or do things on a grand scale, it's more that they want to do things the way they think they should be done. And if that means doing things elaborately and spending money, then they're prepared to do it. But some of the things we do for Duran Duran are very straightforward. The thing is, they acknowledge the importance of quality and presentation.

In the case of Duran Duran, different members of the band make different contributions to the process, I suspect . . .

MG: Yes. So you have to constantly weigh up the relative importance of schemes and thoughts so that they have to have the final trust in your decision when it comes to what you actually do. If you have six or seven different thoughts on the same matter, at the end of the day one person's got to say, well I think this is the right way of doing it.

● Seven And The Ragged Tiger

So you have to capture the spirit of the band.

MG: Yes. You have to override some personal thoughts for the good of the group.

Yes, but what does a graphic designer actually do? I mean, how do these images, these ideas . . .

MG: Quite a lot of the time he just sits and talks . . . Another part of the time he sits with a photographer and takes pictures. Another part of the time he sits and draws. He also sits pondering over pages and pages of typed copy, or argues with his friendly computer, or sweats it out in the darkroom. Still later he pulls all the information he's got together from those enterprises and attempts to make some manageable whole, which he then has to deliver to the printer. So he spends part of his time with platemakers transferring the collated information into print, and then he might spend part of this time in a factory overseeing the production run of a sleeve or book or whatever.

So only part of his time is actually spent drawing.

MG: In fact maybe only 25 per cent of the time.

What is it that attracts a designer to pop music?

MG: An interest in pop music.

But aren't there things about pop music which enable you as a graphic designer to develop your ideas more freely than in other fields and express them in the marketplace?

MG: Well, I became involved in it because I like all things visual, and I'm also inspired by music, and on a simple level I saw people were doing record sleeves and I thought I could do it better. On an enormous amount of levels I was very naive about what was actually involved, which is presumably what this piece is trying to clear up. So I got involved because in the early days I couldn't see the future as a pure artist — I mean, there aren't that many Andy Warhols around — but I could see a future for getting visual work printed and used — visual work that I was confident was better than other people's. I therefore acknowledged at quite an early stage that if I was working for someone, then really what I was doing should in the first instance sell the product and not me.

How can you reflect music visually?

MG: That's the eternal question. That's what I have sleepless nights over. You just find that you've done it one day. Explaining what you did to achieve that, you would have to discuss every client's work in detail, to find out how you arrived at specific solutions. It's actually a complementary thing. One's perception of music is coloured by the graphic work done. When you think of the music, part of the perception in your mind is what's on the record sleeve and the visuals surrounding it. And therefore the reverse is also true. When you see the visuals, it means you hear the music. It's just impossible to explain or describe a perception, but everybody knows the feeling. You think of Pink Floyd and you think of **Dark Side Of The Moon,** and you think of that triangle, that prism. And you hear the sound of cash registers. The two have become interlinked in your mind, and this is why the designer working with the band is so important, because you develop that link and you continue to reinforce it with feedback and cross-fertilisation, and the links become . . . Don't ask me how to do it; it happens.

How important is it for the designer to have an empathy for the music that he's working on?

MG: It depends whether the music is that important to what the band's about. *Understanding* is more important than *liking*. I mean, with a band like Throbbing Gristle the music is just an extension of the band as social protagonists. Music is always an extension of what the band are about in real terms. And it's understanding the band and their motives more than necessarily understanding what a particular song is about . . . Your involvement as a designer can be as broad as the band's range of activities, in theory. Graphic design is about conveying information via different media, which logically means you can apply your talents to video, clothing, stage presentation; in fact, wherever information is conveyed visually.

Peter Saville (designer with Ultravox, New Order, OMD) says he doesn't like music, doesn't listen to it much.

MG: Yes, that's lies. He knows what New Order are about. He's helped create them.

Are designers currently 'in vogue' and will they go out of vogue at some time?

MG: I don't think that's possible. It's a bit like saying, is advertising in vogue? When advertising started to happen post-war — you know, the Madison Avenue theory of advertising — people realised its importance. And now, you cannot sell a new soft drink without an advertising campaign . . . Or it's like, are producers in vogue? Particular producers will come in and out of vogue for their particular styles and talents, but the theory that a band needs their sound produced won't go away. Even bands that want to get back to a primitive sound, a 'non-produced' sound, that's still an aspect of production. You cannot relinquish knowledge. You cannot regain naivety.

Do you think particular designers are in fashion and will go out of fashion?

MG: There have been particular designers in vogue. I mean, Pete lives on a knife edge (ha, ha). Jamie Reid was a kind of semi-designer very much in vogue and now, sadly, that work is just recognised as a style.

So it depends whether a designer is identified with an individual style or not.

MG: Quite so. Assorted iMaGes has no style . . . you might say.

What are you own favourite pieces of work?

MG: Well . . . the Simple Minds cover for a start, because so many people hate it. It has as much effect being disliked as it did being liked. It polarised opinion — no press is bad press and all that . . . I like different pieces of my work for different reasons. But we can come back to that one.

● Sparkle In The Rain

● Movement

FACE TO ƎƆⱯℲ

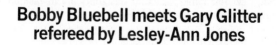

Bobby Bluebell meets Gary Glitter
refereed by Lesley-Ann Jones

A gleaming, steaming Saturday mid-way through June and I, for one, am sporting the hangover of the year (courtesy of Capital Radio, Thomas Dolby and EMI Records — must stick to one party a night in future). Old Pink Eyes is back . . . there is but one thing for it. Ever seen a bald dog?

Shielded by a pair of old and faithful Ray-Bans, I venture gingerly along Camden Passage; past stall-loads of junk jewels, yellowing lace and silver spoons looking for a mouth to be born in, to Frederick's Restaurant. I claim my table in the Garden Room — and wait.

A delightfully cool and airy glass construction, the elegant extension brims with lush green foliage, somewhat reminiscent of a Kew Gardens hot-house. Widely respected as one of London's better restaurants, Frederick's is delicious, extravagant, smart . . . not often graced with the presence of unruly (and that's putting it mildly) characters from the dubious world of rock and pop. The setting is classy, the clientèle well-off, the wines fine and the cuisine — well, more of that later. I am more concerned for the safety of my absent guest stars. At such times, panic strikes and fingers tremble. Only laid-back journalists a little long in the tooth ever feel capable of relaxing in their seats and ordering a top-up of the Bollinger bucket. I am too fidgety to indulge, and what bothers me is the obvious: will they turn up? Worse than that, did they even *wake* up? After all, it *is* Saturday . . .

I need not have worried. At 1.30pm precisely, the door swings open and younger heads turn in recognition of one Robert Hodgens Esq. — he of the lank locks, unglamorous garb and ubiquitous Ray-Bans. He wears the broadest of smiles, as always; gabbles away in thick Glaswegian and wades into the alcohol. Bobby Bluebell knows how to make himself at home.

Half an hour and two (nearly three) bottles later, cutlery clatters to a halt and all ears twitch at the sound of those inimitable dulcet tones. Extending a hand to all and sundry, Paul Gadd makes his flamboyant entrance with a shrill and bemused *"What time of morning do you call this, Jones?"* In a baggy black track suit and — you've guessed it — Ray-Bans, he looks smaller, even younger, minus the sequins and the platform boots. In spite of that, there is not a face in the place who does not recognise Gary Glitter.

Glitter meets Bluebell and the champagne corks fly — literally. Bobby and Gary greet each other as old friends, and nobody else gets a word in edgeways. Menus are fumbled with and glasses refilled as beaming photographer Duncan snaps away regardless. Oblivious to the camera, our pair of pop stars chatter on. Age separates them to the tune of twenty years. Music is music and it's all rock and roll to them — but what on earth do these two have in common? Much more than meets the eye, it seems.

Read on.

Gary: *(Making self comfortable, wriggling bottom in seat and knocking head against wall — mine — grabs menu).* I've starved myself all week. I even cancelled the Virgin Atlantic flight for this.' *(Laughs and reveals gold teeth in abundance.)* Aren't you impressed?

Bobby: Nope. I've been up all night. We were playing at 3 o'clock this morning. No, don't ask me to take my glasses off. You'll regret it.

Gary: What are you, then . . . a sight for sore eyes? *(Smirk, giggle.)* Is that *so?* *(Hands on hips.)* What do you think of this lot? *(Extends hand and shows off wrist adorned with unusual selection of bracelets).* See this black rubber bangle . . . I got it in New York. Kinky, eh? What do you mean, plastic on elastic? This one was three hundred quid from Woolies.

Bobby: You look like a gipsy in that lot.

Gary: You've got to be a gipsy in this business. It's all to do with my ever-changing moods! And enthusiasm, of course. When I've been away on tour, the minute I get back home I want to be out on the road again. I'm a hard task-master — unto myself! And I'm a drama queen 24 hours a day.

Bobby: You can say that again. I remember reading about you being on *Ready Steady Go* in the early days — what was all that about?

Gary: I was a sort of programme assistant — in about 1965. Yeah — I was about 25. You would have been about five. Not a lot in it now, though, eh? I got away with murder in those days. Well . . . it was an experience.

Bobby: And ever since then you've been making comebacks.

Gary: Cheeky sod!

Bobby: Why did you change your name to Gary Glitter?

Gary: I might ask you the same question.

Bobby: But my name's not Gary Glitter!

Gary: Alright, alright! Well, why's it Bluebell?

Bobby: Simply because the bluebell is the national flower of Scotland, as well as being my favourite flower. That and the poppy.

Gary: Ooh, really? Mine's the rose. I used to throw roses to my public. I like gardenias, too. They smell lovely. But we digress. *(Swigs another throatful of champagne).* Listen, if there's champagne to be drunk, I'll drink it. Why the hell not is what I say. I became Gary Glitter because it went with whole glitter rock craze that was happening at the time. Me and this guy, Mike Leander, who was my manager at the time — I think — created this — character, I suppose you'd call it — and that was me. The music part just followed on from there. I had 11 UK top ten hits and three Number Ones between '72 and '75. Not bad, eh? That, my dears, was my heyday. *(Launches into song).* DO you wanna touch . . . DO you wanna touch . . . Lesley's looking worried . . . Don't panic, love, just pass the bottle! I've had my share of problems too . . . I went bankrupt and did my five years' penance . . .

Bobby: And now you're making *another* comeback. I really love your new song *Dance Me Up.*

Gary: Yeah, not bad, is it? Video's great too, innit? I had a lot of fun doing that.

Bobby: Say no more.

Gary: *(Raises glass)* Cheers, mate. *(Hugs all round. Forkful of Glitter's pasta falls into Bluebell's melon — which Bluebell complains is too hard to eat. Either that or his teeth are too soft.)* How did you get into this lark, anyway?

Bobby: What, this lunch? Well Lesley-Ann just rang me up and invited me . . .

Gary: No, you berk, I mean the music business.

Bobby: Oh, that, Well, it's quite simple and painless, really. I was writing for a local fanzine when I left school. There have always been a lot of groups in Glasgow to write about! My contempories were — and are — people like Aztec Camera and Orange Juice . . . I went to Art School for a bit, but that was quite boring. Anyway, everyone was into forming groups, and late in 1979, I think it was, I got together with Ken and Dave (McCluskey — brothers) and a couple of others who have since left, and formed the Bluebells. We did loads of gigs, and eventually came down to London and impressed lots of people! We signed to London Records in 1982. A string of wildly wonderful, quirky pop singles sounding like a cross between the Byrds and the Monkees — I was always a great fan of the Monkees — got us absolutely nowhere. At the beginning we all sported matching white Levi jackets, and looked like something out of a surfing movie! We finally made it this spring with *I'm Falling.*

Gary: Yeah, I'm mad for that song. I think it's terrific.

Bobby: Well, thank *you,* hen!

Gary: I love the new one, too. *(Launches into song again)* Young at heart, young at heart . . . doo be doo be doo — I quite like Frank Sinatra too, by the way.

Bobby: I'm glad about that.

Gary: You said you were really keen on the Monkees.

Bobby: Yeah — I'm a believer! When I was about eight or nine, we formed a Monkees Club at my School. Then when I was a bit older, Marc Bolan arrived on the scene. He really captured my imagination. I idolised the man. T-Rex, the Monkees, Rolling Stones, Mott the Hoople . . . they were all my favourite bands. The first record I ever bought was Bolan's *Ride A White Swan,* in 1971. It was a stunning record — still is.

Gary: I agree. *(Leaps to his feet).* A toast, everyone, *(at the top of his voice — all heads in the restaurant turn)* to Marc Bolan. Where is he? You still do a song of theirs in your set, don't you?

Bobby: Yeah — *Hot Love.* That's my other favourite. What was the first record you ever bought, Gary?

Gary: *(Without hesitation)* It was a long time ago, but I can remember the day I went out and got it. It

was Elvis Presley's *Paralysed* – in 1957! Elvis had a great effect on my life. He was probably the biggest influence on me – after my Uncle John, who used to come round and play the guitar. You know, all those Hank Williams-type licks. He was a winner, an' all! Remember Elvis in *Loving You?* That was a brilliant film. And *Jailhouse Rock* and what was the other one, *King Creole?* That was a bit of alright. After that, he went off. Or I went off *him* – one of the two! Talking of Elvis, you supported Elvis Costello in '82, didn't you?

Bobby: Yeah – it was magnificent. The legendary Imperial Bedroom Tour of Britain. I'll not forget that in a hurry. He's produced us a bit, too. Nice bloke.

Gary: Certainly is. Waiter! Champagne! Service! Can you *hear* me over there, young man? What is it I'm having for main course . . . a slice of goat. Oh – a slice of goat's *cheese...* now you're talking. Life has become so confusing ever since I converted to vegetarianism.

Bobby: We know what you mean.

Gary: So what do you think of the music business, then, Bobby?

Bobby: I think it's all terribly contradictory, to tell you the truth. I mean, all the groups in the charts at the moment are quite conservative, aren't they – even though this is supposed to be the age when anything goes. Everyone aspires to being rich . . . and there are no groups who are socially aware. It's all apathy these days, too. Not like Marc Bolan's day. I mean, look at him. He *was* the seventies. Nothing apathetic about him. But I *am* glad to be making music for a living. It's a great luxury to be able to tell the world how you feel through a song. Some people might think we just write silly pop songs – but there is a meaning in them thar lyrics!

Gary: I believe you! It's a topsy turvy world though, music, innit? I mean, Trevor Horn once played bass for me! Look at him now! You know, in the sixties it was all black and white and everyone knew where they stood and who cares? Now it's all got to be cosmic and meaningful. Spandau Ballet and groups like them are just like the Osmonds, really, when you think about it. They're just rehashing what the Ossies did, and the way they were. They have exactly the same effect on the kids. Bring back David Cassidy, that's what I say! He and Donny Osmond will be remembered forever. And her, whatsername . . . Marie. *(Launches into another song)* Paper Woses . . . Paper Woses . . . la la la la la . . . But what did you used to want to be when you left school? Not a musician, surely?

Bobby: You're right. I wanted to be a painter. Infact, I *really* wanted to be Andy Warhol, or Picasso. Warhol's really rich – that's another reason why I wanted to be him. I *love* money. It comes from growing up quite poor.

Gary: Tell me about it. I was illegitimate, and brought up in an orphanage. Imagine the difference it made to me. That's why I had to spend it all so quick!

Bobby: I also longed for the guts to steal other people's ideas, like so many people do. That would be great. To be a cross between really rich and really talented would be wonderful. I'd be the musical Marlon Brando and James Dean rolled into one. If I wasn't in a band now, I'd rather like to be in TV. I adore John Pilger, and I'd quite like to tackle a war programme or two. It all fascinates me.

Gary: Well, when I grow up I'd like to be a train driver. No, really . . . since doing videos I'd quite like to act or direct full-time. OK, it's weeks of headache for a three minute splash, but it's worth it. It's great. But music is my first love. *(Addresses entire restaurant — everyone by this time enchanted).* We're all fans of each other, folks. In this business, we don't get bored. Take note! You might think we do, but we don't really. We *love* music. You've just got to keep tuning in to the youth of today. And they're quite happy to be plugged into, believe me! People who think they know it all may as well give up now. The older you get, the more you've got to listen.

Bobby: The younger you are, the more you've got to listen to older people. Not just the musicians who've been doing it for ten or twenty years, but people from all walks of life. It puts things in perspective. I read a lot of biographies for that reason. The ones that most impressed me were the Kennedys and the Kray Twins. Don't ask me why.

Gary: Okay, we won't. By the way, don't ever forget to be as enthusiastic as you are now. It's *very* important. I remember at University – not that I ever went to one, but still . . . everyone did bugger all. You *need* to be enthusiastic in life. You can never be sure that anyone will want to hear what you have to say, but you must say it anyway. You must express your feelings, and if you can, be a genius! It helps. Look at Paul McCartney. He's one. But he doesn't understand his own brilliance. He says something in a song and all the intellectuals go 'Wallop!' And *he* says 'Where?' But that's not too important. You don't have to be able to read something in yourself, or in your work, for it to be there. If the *customer* sees it, then it's there alright. What's your favourite hobby, Bobby . . . good bit of poetry that, innit?

Bobby: Fabulous! Actually, I really love football. But it's dying out – just like pop music. By 1990 there'll be no football and no singles. The two go hand in hand. So, from my point of view, it's good to get in now – at the end. Technology's killing everything off. Creativity and personality hardly count anymore. Sad . . . but there's nothing we can do about it. Just hope it all stays together long enough for our kids to see what it was like.

Gary: You like kids?

Bobby: Yeah – other people's! In ten years' time I'll probably get married and have dozens of them – doesn't everyone? That's the whole point of life, after all – to procreate. Go forth and multiply.

Gary: Not right this minute, thanks – but I know what you mean. Anyway, I've done all that. I've already got mine, thanks. My boy's 20 and my daughter's 19, so I leave them to get on with it. That's something you'll have to remember, when the time comes – don't cramp their style, and they'll thank you for it.

Bobby: I'll bear it in mind!

(The equivalent of a bathful of strawberries arrives, accompanied by deep basins of sugar and cream. Inebriated guests dive in — almost head-first)

Gary: Champagne! I've got a song . . .*(leaps to feet)*

The restaurant's bad
The food's not bad
The company's even better.
But then we should find
Ourselves inclined
to . . . what rhymes with better?

Bobby: Don't ask. What about a nice *Scottish* song.

Gary: *(In trouser-splitting soprano)* Speed bonny boat . . . like a bird on the WING . . .

Bobby: *(Tenor)* Over the sea to Skye . . .

Gary: You can do better than that.

Bobby: I certainly can. Ye'll tak the high road and I'll tak the low road . . .

Gary: And I'll be in Scotland afore ye . . .

(It is now nearly 5 pm. The entire restaurant has emptied. Gary is unperturbed.)

Gary: *(Jazz-style)* There's only one Gadd and there's only one Bob, so let's just pretend we're a couple of slobs . . .

Bobby: Who's pretending?

Gary: I *love* being an actress. I just *know* you're wondering 'How does the old bastard do it?'

Hang-ups? I don't have hang-ups. I lived with a gay painter once, and every now and again I let him touch my shoulders. That was about it as far as hang-ups go.

Bobby: Surely you can't be serious . . .

Gary: Don't call me Shirley . . .

Bobby: *Very* old joke . . .

Gary: *(Resting head against very rough brick wall)* Would anyone mind telling me what I did between 1972 and 1976? There are enough books about it, but I just never get around to reading any of them.

Bobby: Tell you what — I'll go home and look it all up; then we can meet again, and get drunk again, and I'll put you straight.

Gary: Cheers. What do you hope for most in life?

Bobby: That I don't get older or fatter or wiser, and that my shoes never change from a size eight. You?

Gary: Oh, I just hope that I don't have to spend the rest of my life fighting flab. Talking of shoes, I take a size six — but I've got a big nose.

Bobby: What's that got to do with it?

Gary: *(Pointing at me)* Ask her. She's paying the bill.

The drunken pair stagger off, arm in arm, into the pale afternoon sunlight. Gary is nursing a broken pair of Ray-Bans. We told him not to fiddle with them. Bobby's faithful and efficient manager, the magnificent Clive Banks, supplies a new pair. "I always keep spares in the car in case of accidents". We know what you mean.

Gary has the last word — or should I say chorus. The cab driver is less than impressed by his rendition of *We'll Meet Again*, but it's passable. They don't call him Vera for nothing.

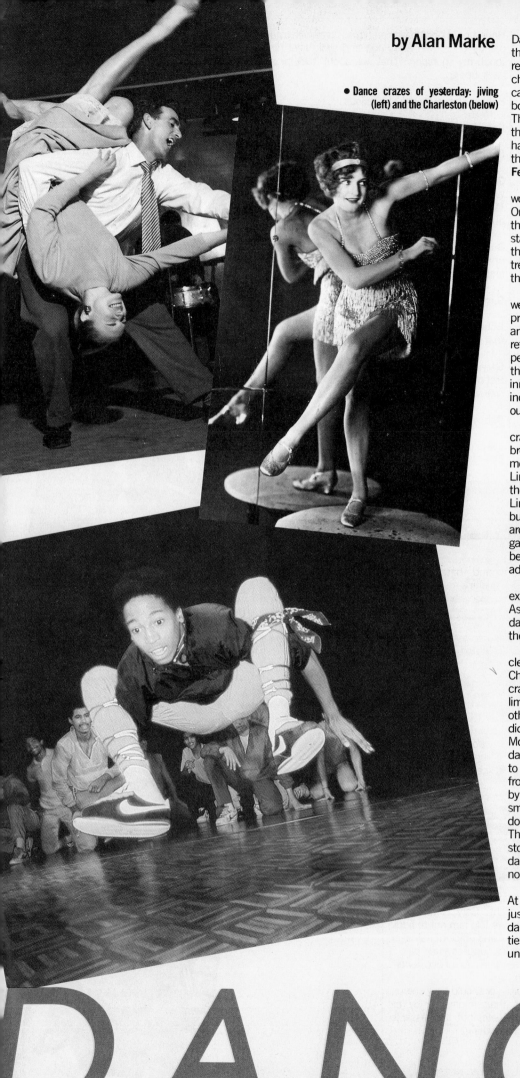

by Alan Marke

● Dance crazes of yesterday: jiving (left) and the Charleston (below)

Dance music has never been as popular amongst the pop-consuming public as in 1984. Half the records that have slid in and out of the UK singles charts this year have had one thing in common. You can dance to them. But what's dance? A bedroom bop, a disco bar shuffle or a dancefloor dervish. The high priest of dance, Michael Jackson, is now the world's biggest selling act. Jackson's **Thriller** LP has reached over 30 million households, outselling the previous world beating set **Saturday Night Fever,** and proving that dance fever has no cure.

The first dance craze to sweep the Western world was the waltz, way back in the early 1800's. Once the big bands of the Victorian age struck up their first chords, couples grabbed each other and started whirling around while counting one, two, three to themselves and concentrating on not treading on toes. This lasted for nearly a century, thanks largely to the lack of records, radios and TV.

Next came the first slave influence. A fusion of western masters' music and African heritage produced dance sensations like the Tango, Rumba, and Samba. Followed by the less intimate and refined Foxtrot. A dance designed for the less permissive society. The unshackled slaves had by the twenties established themselves as the main innovative group in western music and the indigenous black sound of jazz produced the outrageous, wriggling, bouncing Charleston.

During the dance marathons, held in the dance crazy Depression times, contestants started to break away, doing their own thing to break up the monotony. The first solo innovation was the Lindy-hop, which was an excuse to do anything to the fast driving jazz of the big bands. The Lindy-hop developed into the more stylised Jitter-bug, which involved couples flinging themselves around with gay abandon. The Jitterbug import gave birth to jiving in the British halls. Jiving became institutionalised and mellow until the advent of rock'n'roll in the 1950's.

Presley's pelvic thrusts turned jiving into an explicitly sexual act and mass hysteria broke out. As the fifties came to an end, sex began to leave the dance floor as couples split up and grooved away in their own private worlds.

The sanitised era of the early sixties saw clean-cut corny ballads clean-up the charts. Chubby Checker's jungle-like Twist was the next big craze. Discotheques flourished, filling up with limbo dancing teenagers trying to out twist each other. Couples seldom touched while twisting, nor did they during the following Mod era. Pill-popping Mods twitched away to the convulsive Caribbean dance sounds of Ska and Blue-beat, which began to mix with the more traditional rhythm'n'blues from the USA. The swinging sixties was dominated by black soul, from the raw Stax sound to the smooth slick Tamla Motown beat. Rock began to dominate the scene in the shape of the Beatles, The Who and Rolling Stones, and as the sixties stopped swinging teenagers seemed to cease dancing and stand transfixed by the mystifying noise of the supergroups.

Disco-dancing began to die as drugs took over. At your local happening, crazed individuals would just freak out with no particular style. The idiot dance continued to be popular during the seventies, although there had always remained an underground soul movement. These keen haters of

DANCE

rock followed their black heroes, James Brown, Sly Stone, George Clinton, Isaac Hayes, Curtis Mayfield, War and more.

Skinheads would shuffle and skank to rude-boy reggae, later the suedeheads might lend an ear to the teeny-bop Jackson 5 and the commercial string-dominated sounds of Barry White, Stylistics, Tavares and the sound of Philadelphia.

During the mid-seventies another recession began and there was a slow general move back to dancing. In northern England dance marathons attracted mad devotees to fast, pumping soul from the Southern States of America. Ridiculously baggy dressed soul fans would jitterbug to forgotten sounds all through the night.

New York saw the real re-birth of disco, as the gay community 'came-out' in a big way, and hundreds of discos opened overnight. Puerto-Ricans danced to their own salsa, the blacks grooved to soul and gays went mad for anything. *Saturday Night Fever* was the commercial pinnacle of disco in the seventies, and white-suited, medallioned Travolta's emerged everywhere from New Jersey and Rome to Tokyo and Ilford.

Seventies dance crazes were more structured into formation such as the Hustle, and required mass participation. Disco threatened to take over completely as punk tried to kill off boring supergroup rock. The punk 'pogo' was not so much a dance, more like an organised fight formation — the ultimate anti-dance, which was really a more energetic form of the late sixties idiot dance.

The eighties have seen punk rock die out, only to be replaced by black punk-electro music. Black and Hispanic New Yorkers, tired of smooth, sophisticated soul, have developed a hard dance sound based around the synthesised drum machine and the 'scratch' technique of DJ mixing. To accompany the electro sounds, derived from European groups such as Kraftwerk, mixed with the soul dance-beat, the dancers have developed a manic form of jitterbugging. Breaking involves spinning from head, to hands, back and feet in an acrobatic effort to impress and is the most exciting dance craze to emerge for years. Coupled with body-popping, an imitation of how a robot would perform on the dance floor, and scratch-mixing, the whole arena of hip hop (as it is collectively known) has swept the world. The films *Flashdance, Footloose, Breakdance* and *Beat Street* have brought about a mass craze for dancing not seen since *Saturday Night Fever*.

A rival to hip hop in Britain has been the latest trend back to jazz. Up and down the country there have been regular jazz nights in clubs previously only catering for disco. Many young jazz fans have created a free-form kind of lindy-hopping crossed with breaking, as they compete with each other to dance to jazz.

There seems to be no stopping the world-beating Michael Jackson, and as soul, jazz and electro fuse, dance music has never been more exciting or popular. If you are like me and can't dance, you can just jig about in a corner of your local disco and enjoy the music, while hoping the 'breakers' don't spill your drink!

● Breakdancing never fails to draw the crowds on street corners. Below: scene from Flashdance

TRENDS

BANDS

• Inside a Touring Bus

● by Robin Eggar

• The Stones at Wembley '82

Remember that climactic concert? That moment of total triumph locked in perpetual stasis in your memory banks? A swashbuckling Adam Ant, a melancholy Sting, a Bowie chameleon in mid-change, a Johnny Rotten in mid-spit, all stuck in a permanant freeze frame.

Video cannot do that. It only shows the same two dimensional image *ad infinitum, ad nauseam.* Video will suck the magic out of Merlin's guitar and package it up like cornflakes, so that the wrapping is as nourishing as the contents.

You cannot beat a live gig. Not even when the band play note for note perfect copies of the record you already know by heart. Not even when the vital words come in machine gun bursts of unintelligibility through a wall of hisses, buzzes and white noise.

Rock music — with all its offshoots, antecedents, categories, call them what you will — has never been a cerebral thing. It should move the feet first, the heart second and the head last. It is music to dance to, to shake to, to scream with — a spectator sport.

The video age has brought about a change. Time was when every bar in Manhattan had a live group vying for attention with White Russians and Screwdrivers. Now it is all discos, videos and concert stadiums. (Although even the gay discos are throwing up bands like the Balls — the Big Apple's answer to Bronski Beat).

No record deal-less band, from the Mid West or Manchester, will set off in a battered van to see the world from Wigan to Washington any more. They cannot afford it. Touring is expensive. There is little profit in it even for the superstars. Profit comes from those hidden extras — like that £5 T shirt, or £3 programme.

That is where the money lies touring. Earlier in the year Duran Duran set a record at Los Angeles' Hollywood Bowl — the kids spent, on average, 10 dollars each on merchandise. When Culture Club left the stage in Tokyo, the merchandising booths were protected by samurai security men facing 10,000 desperate teenies, yen in hand.

The Rolling Stones make money on the road, but only because they can fill 50,000 seaters wherever they find them. On the '82 European tour it cost them £250,000 per week just to stand still.

The saviour of touring, the vital bottom line addition to the account books, *may* be corporate sponsorship. In the UK, Guinness have sponsored The Police, Levi Jeans David Bowie and Roxy Music, and Sony Tapes (just slipping this in, honest!) Duran Duran. In America it is a much bigger ballgame, from the reputed three and a half million dollars Pepsi Cola have put behind the

Jacksons to the hundred thousand Coca Cola gave Duran — which they promptly spent on a giant video screen.

Certainly, at the moment, it is the biggies who gain. But perhaps sponsorship will help remove one of the great touring rip offs, practiced since time immemorial on the chaps who can afford it least — the support band.

What a confidence trick it was. The support band would pay anything from £1000 to £7000, depending on the status and length of the tour, for the dubious privilege of being ignored by the crowd. The sound and lights crew of the headliner would then extract their pounds of flesh as well. The support band were always paid — fifty quid a night.

Small wonder that Duran Duran slept in their van when supporting Hazel O'Connor.

Despite such iniquities touring is fun. It is also insufferably boring. The two are inextricably interwoven.

● The Police

● David Bowie

The best times are generally the hardest. Police guitarist Andy Summers remembers the tiny gigs better than the football stadiums.

"In the early days, Stewart and I used to run around London sticking up posters. Then we'd borrow a van — which would always break down — which we'd end up pushing to the gig. Then the PA would cost us £70 for the night and our fee would be £75. Now we earn a quarter of a million bucks a show and they are all the same."

Take the Members — a London based punk band who had two hits in 1979 with **Sound Of The Suburbs** and **Off-Shore Banking Business**. They toured consistently on a shoestring. They got to travel the world, meet (and sometimes sleep with) interesting people, and unlike the army, they did not have to kill anyone.

Mind you, it was close sometimes. In Edinburgh the singer was nearly decapitated by a guitar; the bass player leapt out of the van at a Bradford traffic lights and vanished, only re-appearing after a spell recuperating in hospital.

The shows could be interesting. One October night in Dover, New Jersey, the audience was only three men and a dog — he didn't like the show either — as the rest of America was watching the deciding game in the World Series. Or in Auckland, New Zealand, where the crowd — who had never seen a punk band before — built a bonfire in the middle of the hall. Or the Crystal Ballroom in Melbourne, where the top floor was haunted and even legendary roadie The Pig refused to tread.

Being places was OK, but the travelling was mind numbing. It is the same with a private jet, or seven crammed in an estate car. There is so much waiting around, before the stage is ready for a sound check. When everyone is happy with the way they sound, they wait some more, sometimes for eight hours. Then they hit the stage for those few minutes of glory or debacle.

And when it's over, even with the sweat ankle deep inside the boots, the adrenalin is still flowing and the musicians have come alive in places that have just died.

It is the boredom that drives groups to smash up hotels. If you've stayed in the same Holiday Inn

room in 43 consecutive towns and there is nothing on the TV except a re-run of *I Love Lucy,* it is tempting to throw a beer bottle at the screen, or carefully unscrew every piece of furniture so that the next hapless occupant suffers a cruel and unnatural punishment.

On the road even casual sex can get debased. Legends of Van Halen's tour manager spotting likely looking blondes in the audience and issuing them with ALL ACCESS — guess what that means — passes are invariably true. One English band held a competition to see who could sleep with the ugliest girl — they called it the Kennel Club!

That isn't very funny for anyone reading it in cold print. But then touring does not bear much resemblance to the reality known to ordinary mortals. It is not surprising that after years crammed up together Roger Daltrey and Pete Townshend of The Who do not like each other at all.

Relationships crack on the road. Few musicians, faced with a free run in the candy store, will turn down the goods on offer. Amazingly, most reject any form of stimulant or narcotic, including booze, before going on stage. Afterwards is another matter…

● The Members on stage

It is a different world on the road. A bubble with its own rules, eccentricities and dangers. The day is an unfolding ritual culminating in the long walk to the stage. The man who throughout the day has resembled the half dead is suddenly vibrant with life.

And for just a few moments, maybe, just maybe, his performance sears itself onto the memory banks. With each recall the taste, the smell, the energy are remembered too.

So you keep going back to rock concerts hoping for another memory. Again and again. And again.

Can video do that?

A GUIDE TO THE LATEST RECORD COLLECTING MANIA
by Phil Swern

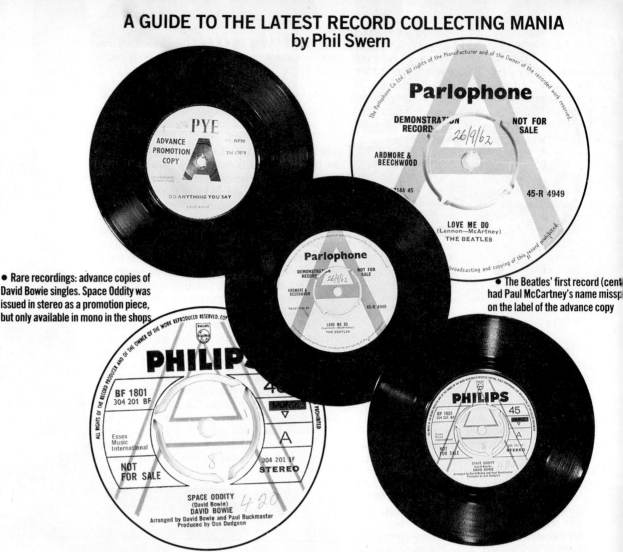

● Rare recordings: advance copies of David Bowie singles. Space Oddity was issued in stereo as a promotion piece, but only available in mono in the shops

● The Beatles' first record (cent[...] had Paul McCartney's name missp[...] on the label of the advance copy

What makes one particular record so collectable? Why do collectors become so obsessed with what started out as a mere hobby? Why does a person who decides to collect all Des O'Connor's records suddenly become like a man possessed, paying fortunes for white label demos, promotion copies, acetates, bootlegs or even foreign pressings of a record that they already own on British release?

The phenomenon is not easily explained. I know, for I am one of the thousands of hardened, incurable record collectors in Britain alone — and there are probably millions throughout the world.

Record collecting really came into its own in the mid-seventies, when enthusiasts became as boring to their friends when they came across a pressing with the original catalogue number, as a train spotter catching a glimpse of the ZE1097983 express arriving at Paddington station. I met a collector once who had just paid £60 for a rare Jim Reeves album and he told me he would never play it for fear of damaging his prize.

There are many collectors who only collect one particular artist, but will buy the same record in as many different forms as they can find: triangular centre, round centre, no centre; seven, 10 or 12 inch copy. They will buy multiple copies of a record that has been pressed in several different countries purely for the different catalogue or matrix numbers. Several of the larger record companies now press their records in one factory and then distribute it worldwide, so there is no longer any reason for the collector to obtain overseas pressings of his favourite artist.

However, a large proportion of independent labels do not have parent companies abroad and therefore make direct deals with foreign dis-tributors, which means that the overseas pressings of their material will still be collectable in years to come.

In reality a record is as valuable as is the need for the collector to own it. An original London American label of **One Night/Ain't Gonna Do It** by Smiley Lewis, would fetch £100 in mint condition. The two songs could be available on a compilation album for a fiver, but a collector of original London American pressings would find the very idea grotesque.

Records made by stars under other names before they hit the big time are of great interest to collectors. Freddy Mercury of Queen recorded a version of **I Can Hear Music,** under the name Larry Lurex, and this is now worth at least £40. Slade recorded **You Better Run** as the 'N'Betweens, but you'd be lucky to get it for under £60. The Who, calling themselves The High Numbers, recorded **I'm The Face:** this is worth £75, but only with the original Fontana label pressing.

Gary Glitter recorded as Paul Raven, Paul Monday and Rubber Bucket; Billy Joel played on records by The Hassels and Attila; Sonny and Cher used the name Caesar and Cleo. There are hundreds of pre-fame records about, some worth more than others. The place to find one of these oddities is at one of the numerous record fairs now held all over the country. Barely does a weekend pass without at least half a dozen of these events being held somewhere in Britain, and now there is an International Fair in Paris lasting three days.

Second hand record shops have become a growth industry. Collectors come from all over the country to track down that elusive piece of vinyl. One guy was collecting all the British hits of 1974 in a foreign language; another wanted every record that Hal Blaine has played drums on (that could amount to thousands as he is one of America's leading session players). People collect one artist, one label or one producer (Joe Meek is probably the most collectable in the latter category, having produced Tom Jones, John Leyton, The Tornadoes, Gene Pitney, Gene Vincent, Tommy Steele and Mike Berry, to name but a few).

Picture discs and coloured vinyl are more recent collectable items. Mainly as a promotional gimmick, record companies in the late seventies started producing a glut of picture discs and odd shaped records in limited editions so that fans would rush out and buy a copy as soon as it was released, and this would put the recording in the charts. The practice has mostly died out, but many of the early picture discs are now changing hands for vast sums.

The question that is always asked is, what is the

released around 1963, is an album called **The Beatles and Frank Ifield,** with the fab four on one side and yodelling Frank on the other — every home should have one!

Mistakes on record labels or sleeves, or even within the pressing will induce a collector to open his wallet eagerly. The Beatles' first British hit, **Love Me Do,** had Paul's surname spelt McArtney on the DJ's promotion copies, which has now sent the price through the ceiling. The initial pressings also had Ringo playing drums, but subsequent copies featured session man Andy White. David Bowie's **The Man Who Sold The World** album first came out with Bowie wearing a very pretty dress on the cover. The record company executives were not amused and insisted the sleeve be changed, thus making the original worth about a hundred pounds.

Singles have been sent out with the wrong B side, albums with an incorrect running order or tracks missing, sometimes even a totally different

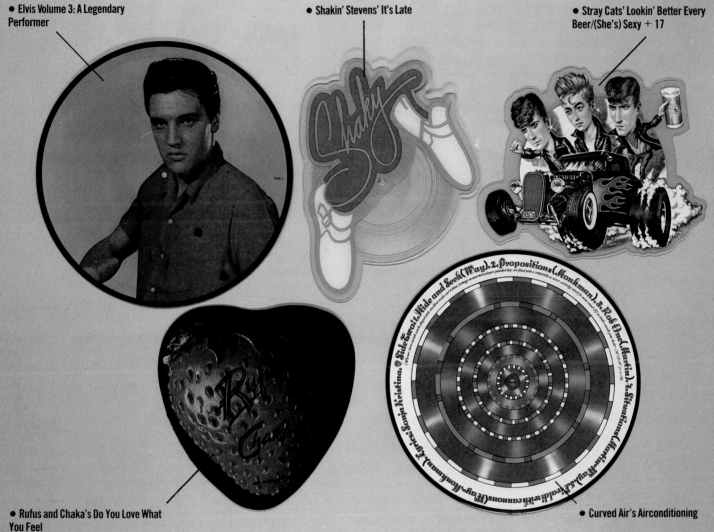

• Elvis Volume 3: A Legendary Performer

• Shakin' Stevens' It's Late

• Stray Cats' Lookin' Better Every Beer/(She's) Sexy + 17

• Rufus and Chaka's Do You Love What You Feel

• Curved Air's Airconditioning

most valuable record in the world? This is impossible to answer though it is generally felt that it would be one of Elvis Presley's more rare recordings. An early interview, which included some songs from an American TV show, was pressed for promotional purposes in the fifties, and the price of one of these is claimed to run into four figures.

The original American pressing of the Presley film *Soundtrack to Speedway,* for some inexplicable reason, can fetch close to a thousand pounds.

Another American oddity of great value

artist to the one named on the label. All these items are highly collectable.

My personal favourites are "the dross", the name I give to novelty records and recordings by actors, sportsmen, disc jockeys and anyone else who should have stuck to what they were good at. These aren't worth much, but are great fun to collect.

Collecting records, though time-consuming, is very rewarding, but be warned...It may seem like a good idea in the beginning, but you can get totally hooked and end up spending a fortune.

OHMS
AN APPRECIATION OF
HEAVY METAL

by Alan Freeman

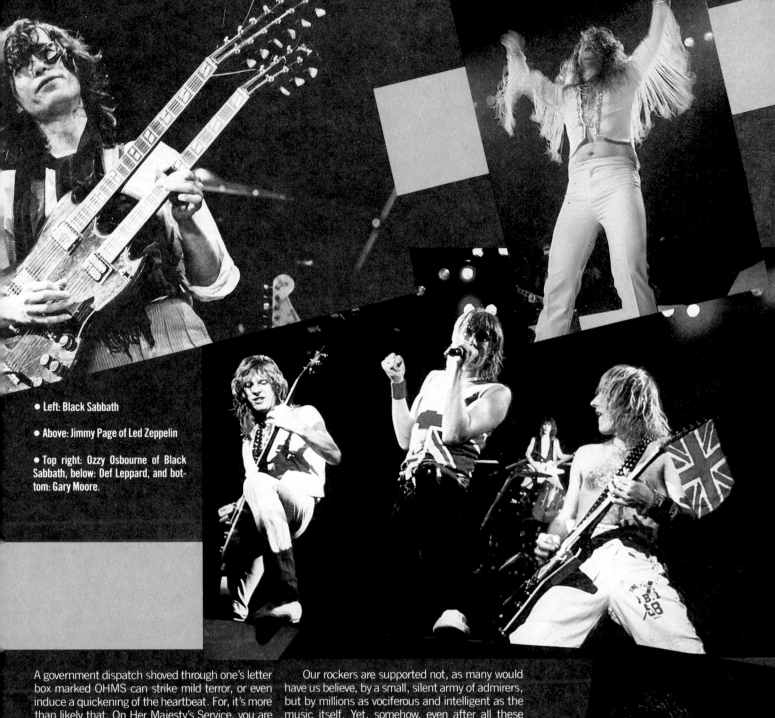

• Left: Black Sabbath

• Above: Jimmy Page of Led Zeppelin

• Top right: Ozzy Osbourne of Black Sabbath, below: Def Leppard, and bottom: Gary Moore.

A government dispatch shoved through one's letter box marked OHMS can strike mild terror, or even induce a quickening of the heartbeat. For, it's more than likely that, On Her Majesty's Service, you are being reminded by the Inland Revenue that all you've managed to accumulate through the sweating of the brow and the agility of the brain is not totally your own property, and some of the cash must be returned to sender.

However, be not alarmed – because this dispatch demands the return of none of your worldly possessions, not even your prized Def Leppard **Pyromania** album. So breathe easily and be assured that this time around, we're engaged On Heavy Metal Service!

Curiously enough, the part of the music industry labelled 'heavy' or progressive rock at its beginning, gradually progressed to what is now termed 'heavy metal'. It is represented around the world by a legion of highly intelligent performers skilled in their respective crafts, who remain intent on spreading a rock music gospel, that deals not just in heavy love-making innuendoes, but feels the need to communicate and even preach to its devotees on a wider series of topics like injustice, political intrigue and, especially, the threat of an impending holocaust that would silence them as well as the rest of us.

Our rockers are supported not, as many would have us believe, by a small, silent army of admirers, but by millions as vociferous and intelligent as the music itself. Yet, somehow, even after all these years, the heavy metal syndrome is still looked upon as a strange, mysterious corner of the music scene, that isn't really family entertainment despite the fact that its growth is enormous!

I remember in the sixties when I was Jock for the Beeb's *Pick Of The Pops*, how I used to listen to John Peel after I came off the air, and how the more I listened, the more I longed to slip a few of those same tracks into *Pick Of The Pops*, rather than just the follow-up singles that were chasing the current middle of the road hits in the top 30.

As time went by, I was able to do this very thing, and that's when I went overboard for the likes of Emerson Lake and Palmer, Jethro Tull, The Who, Cream, Barclay James Harvest, The Nice, Deep Purple and Led Zeppelin. I received a phone call from one of the most energetic pluggers, nay, even 'promotions persons' of the sixties, by the name of Dave Most. He's the brother of Mickie, and week after week, it was Dave who ran up Rak's phone bill as he pointed out the potential of a new Rak single for *Pick Of The Pops*. On this occasion, Dave asked if I'd heard the band Man and their album **Two Ounces Of Plastic With A Hole In The Middle**. I did

HEAVY

● More heavies (from top left): Sammy Hagar, Robert Plant of Led Zeppelin, Lynyrd Skynyrd, and two shots of Motorhead (right)

and eventually got rather carried away by a 12 minute track called **Prelude And Storm** which I played on *Pick Of The Pops* for three successive weeks.

The show from then on became a beautifully weird mixture of pop and heavy rock, and with the feeling that pop would more or less take care of itself, I was quite excited with the prospect of belting some rock/metal to a mass audience, giving even more radio space to those who may be waiting for it.

Ken Dodd singing **Tears,** then Led Zeppelin tearing their hearts out with **Whole Lotta Love** the next minute must have sounded quite strange, but why not? — though I think that to this very day that some of those in charge are still of the opinion that *"never the twain shall meet"*!

When I was taken off *Pick Of The Pops* in 1972, I got even luckier. I had the chance of a lifetime in terms of broadcasting when I was given *The Saturday Rock Show* in association with producer Tony Wilson. Now, we could really get stuck into the heavies with reckless abandon. I was, in truth, the oldest rocker in the world, but did it really matter? We could all unite in the name of heavy metal and drown ourselves in the stimulating music that came from Pink Floyd, Black Sabbath, Lynyrd Skynyrd, The Sensational Alex Harvey Band, Manfred Mann's Earthband, Van Halen, Nils Lofgren, Rush, Queen, Vangelis and a million more.

Meanwhile, a new young generation had been growing up who were influenced by heavies I've mentioned. This new era saw the birth of New Wave and Punk. And if they weren't always musical the "new heavies" smacked of raw rebellion and seemed, if anything, even more aware of injustice and deprivation in the late seventies and early eighties.

There have been and always will be the casualties of each generation of music, but as we head for the middle eighties, most of the old and the new heavies will still be there preaching and pounding their rock metal gospels, and may they never cease!

METAL

As I sit pounding this 'banger' of a typewriter with rather worn fingers, I can report, with the same enthusiasm as when I first encountered Emerson Lake and Palmer, that radio programme patterns in the USA have altered quite dramatically, and that now, the rock metal artistes are having their say en masse, with equal billing to all those who comprise the second British invasion of America and the universe. It's been a long and winding road hasn't it? Most of it unmade road!

I hope these patterns take shape in the UK too, and it's always of great comfort to know that the two most requested tracks on radio stations right around the world are Lynyrd Skynyrd's **Free Bird** and Led Zeppelin's **Stairway To Heaven.**

If by chance you've gazed at all this delirious nonsense, and haven't yet been blinded by the light, can I suggest that you find the inclination and the time to take in some music from the German band Eloy on the Heavy Metal label... and some of Dio's **Holy Diver** album? You might like some Motorhead mayhem, and you really should catch up on what Sammy Hagar and Cast have done to **A Whiter Shade Of Pale** in the eighties. And incidentally, if you've never encountered the superb guitar playing of Gary Moore, then you really haven't lived.

There isn't the slightest doubt in my mind that even Boy George would donate a further chorus to the rock metal cause and chant, *"It's a miracle"*!

The Editors

Lesley-Ann Jones was born in Kent. She studied modern languages in London and Paris and worked in advertising before becoming a freelance journalist in 1980. As well as researching and writing articles, biographies and sleeve notes on various music personalities, and recording freelance radio interviews, she has co-hosted the Channel 4 programme *Earsay*. Her first novel, *Blade On A Mirror,* was published in autumn 1984. and she is now hard at work on her second.

Robin Eggar went straight into the music business from Bristol university as PR for RCA records. He left to manage punk band The Members, then in 1981 turned to freelance journalism working on the daily tabloids, *NME* and *Record Mirror*. He writes a weekly column on the current rock scene for the *Daily Mirror* and is an occasional contributor to the *Sunday Times Colour Supplement, You, The Face* and *Honey*. He has also appeared on BBC2's *Riverside* and *David Jensen's Radio One Evening Show*.

After a successful career in record promotion and production **Phil Swern** began working in radio and television as a writer/ researcher and broadcaster on *You Ain't Heard Nothing Yet, Ear-say,* and *The Rock And Roll Trivia Quiz*. His record collection is one of the largest in the country and consists of every chart single in Britain since 1952. It recently had to be moved out of his house as the vinyl was beginning to take over.

The contributors

David Dorrell (*Depeche Mode, New Order, The Smiths*)
Robin Eggar (*Duran Duran, Frankie Goes To Hollywood, Cyndi Lauper, Sade, Bands On Tour*)
Hugh Fielder (*The Police*)
Alan Freeman (*OHMS*)
Malcolm Garrett (*The Packaging Of Pop*)
Kasper de Graaf (*Culture Club, The Packaging Of Pop*)
Pete Johnson (*Reggae*)
Lesley-Ann Jones (*Spandau Ballet, Imagemakers, Face To Face, Behind The Scenes*)
Joan Komlosy (*Nik Kershaw, Limahl, UB40*)
Alan Marke (*Dance Trends*)
Patrick MacLachlan (*Be A Sport*)
Anne Nightingale (*Evergreens*)
Simon Potter (*Heaven 17, Human League, Wham!, Paul Young*)
Stewart Regan (*Elvis Costello, Michael Jackson, Madness, Lionel Richie, Style Council, Thompson Twins, the Womacks*)
Adam Sweeting (*Big Country, Simple Minds, U2*)
Phil Swern (*Howard Jones, the Pretenders, Rock Roots, Collector's Corner*)
Peter Wagg (*Let The Good Times Roll*)
Johnny Waller (*Eurythmics*)

Rambletree Publishing (Richard Dewing, Michael Forster and Sarie Forster) would also like to thank the following people for their help:

Anne-Marie Ehrlich and David Hare (*Picture research*)
Tristram Woolston and Nick Page of Woolston Design Associates, and Giorgio Moltoni (*Design*)

Thanks to the following photographers and picture libraries:

Keith Altham, Peter Anderson, Allan Ballard, Adrian Boot, Anton Corbijn, David Corio, Fin Costello, Paul Cox, Chris Craymer, Chrysalis, Daily Express, Chris Duffy, Robert Ellis, Simon Fowler, Jill Furmainovsky, Andre Grossman, Hulton Picture Library, Human League, ILPO Music, Island Records, Bob King, David Levine, London Features International, Paramount Pictures Corporation, Duncan Raban, David Redfern, Repfoto, Rex Features, Paul Rider, Scope Features, Skyline Features, Paul Slattery, Still Rock Photography, Syndication International, Eric Watson, WEA.